The CHRISTMAS Book

The Christmas Book

How to Have the Best Christmas Ever

Juliana Foster

Michael O'Mara Books Limited

First published in Great Britain in 2007 by
Michael O'Mara Books Limited
9 Lion Yard
Tremadoc Road
London SW4 7NQ

A CIP catalogue record for this book is available from the British
Library

Papers used by Michael O'Mara Books Limited are natural,
recyclable products made from wood grown in sustainable forests.
The manufacturing processes conform to the environmental
regulations of the country of origin.

ISBN: 978-1-84317-282-6

10 9 8 7 6 5 4 3 2 1

www.mombooks.com

Cover design by Angie Allison from an original design by
www.blacksheep-uk.com

Cover illustration by David Woodroffe

Design by K DESIGN, Winscombe, Somerset

Printed and bound in Great Britain by Clays Ltd, St Ives plc

To Henry

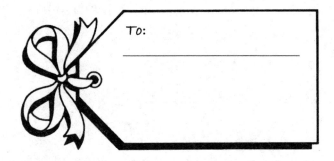

TO:

_____

Contents

Introduction

Christmas is a time for peace on earth and goodwill to all. It is a time for family and friends; sitting in front of a crackling fire; cold, crisp days and fun in the snow; rosy-cheeked children singing carols; the spicy aroma of mulled wine; Christmas trees adorned with twinkling lights . . .

It is also a time for family feuding, overdrafts and angry letters from the bank manager, pretending to like embarrassingly inappropriate gifts, hangovers, turkeys that refuse to defrost, drowning in a mountain of wrapping paper, indigestion, and getting drunk at the office party and snogging the boss.

Whether you're one of life's Scrooges – turning off all the lights and hiding behind the sofa when the carollers come calling, content with an M&S meal-for-one for Christmas lunch, doing all your Christmas shopping at the local pound shop – or whether you throw yourself into the spirit of the season with gusto, a merry 'Ho! Ho! Ho!' escaping from

9

your lips at every opportunity, we all need a bit of a helping hand at Christmas.

Here you can learn how to have the best Christmas ever without breaking a sweat. How to wrap those awkwardly shaped presents, how to choose and care for a tree, how to cope with cooking a meal large enough to feed a small village for a week, how to keep the family entertained when all there is on the telly is yet another *Only Fools and Horses* rerun – it's all to be found within these pages. Satisfy the anorak in you with our comprehensive lists of must-know Christmas facts, from who held the coveted No.1 spot on the singles charts on any given year, to Christmas Day events throughout history, and impress your friends with your knowledge of the origins of all things Christmassy. Full of jokes, tips, trivia, spoof thank-you letters and tales of rampaging Santas, this book is all you'll need to get you through the ups and downs of the festive season.

Hosting a Christmas Party (1)

So you've decided to throw caution to the wind and host your own Christmas bash, and you want the occasion to be a memorable one. Needless to say, this doesn't involve putting on an old Slade album, laying out some cheese on toothpicks and leaving your guests to fend for themselves. Read on for some great tips on how to make sure your party is the one everybody is talking about this year.

Invitations

If you don't want to spend the evening sitting on your own surrounded by enough food to feed an army for a week, make sure you send your invitations out in good time: at least three weeks before the event is advisable during the busy party season.

Be realistic when it comes to your guest list. How many people can your house comfortably accommodate? There's nothing worse than a room crammed full of hot, sweaty guests all shouting at the tops of their voices to make themselves heard and struggling to get anywhere near a plate of nibbles or bottle of wine. Also, what is your budget? It's better to over-cater for your guests than to leave them wanting more, so if you haven't got that much to spend stick to a more intimate gathering of close friends and family. Be aware that inevitably someone will ring at the last minute to ask whether they can bring their brother/aunt/new boyfriend,

11

so make allowances for this when deciding on numbers. Ask people to RSVP and include your phone number and/or email address on your invitations. A few days before the party you should contact anyone who hasn't replied to confirm whether they will be attending.

Invite your immediate neighbours. If you don't get on with them, they probably won't come anyway, but they will appreciate the thought and will be less likely to complain about the noise! If you're adamant that you don't want to invite them, at least warn them that you will be hosting a party and apologize in advance for the inconvenience.

It's always better to mail out invitations rather than sending a round-robin email. People will appreciate the extra care taken and are more likely to RSVP if there is a card sitting on their mantelpiece reminding them to do so. If you

do decide to send a group email, send it to yourself and bcc ('blind carbon copy') your guests, so that their inboxes are not suddenly filled up with irritating 'reply to all' messages. Along with the obvious information – date, timings, your address and so on – include directions (if your home is difficult to find), available parking spots, dress code (if any – see below), phone numbers of a couple of local cab firms and perhaps even details of some local hotels for those guests who may need to travel to attend your party.

Themes

Having a theme for your party can be a great ice-breaker and allows you to be creative with your decorations. Fancy dress can be fun, but remember that not everyone enjoys dressing up as a cowboy/vicar/gorilla etc., and you certainly

don't want to force your guests to spend a lot of money hiring costumes. If you do decide on a fancy-dress party, pick a theme that people can dress for easily using bits and bobs they will already have in their wardrobes, such as 70s, Rock 'n' Roll, Roaring Twenties or Gangsters and Molls. Colour themes are a good alternative to fancy dress. How about a Christmassy red and green theme, or glamorous black and white? Or, even simpler, asking everyone to wear a hat can produce some hilarious results!

Preparing your house

Even if you think your guests are the most well-behaved people on the planet, a little bit of Christmas spirit and a lot of the alcoholic variety mean that breakages and spillages are inevitable. You won't enjoy your party if you're constantly worrying about your precious possessions, so pack away that Persian rug and the Meissen tableware and stash them in an off-limits room – you can show them off some other time. Have a dustpan and brush and a few cloths and cleaning materials ready in a handy place so you can quickly deal with any disasters.

If necessary, rearrange your furniture so that people have room to move around and can get down to a bit of boogying if they wish. If you're worried about spillages on your sofas, chuck a few inexpensive throws over them.

Set up a table in the main party room where you can lay out food and drink. One of your jobs as host is to pass these around, but you don't want to be doing that all night long. If you've got the space, it's a good idea to have various plates of nibbles scattered around the room on small tables so your guests don't have to queue up for a handful of crisps.

If you allow smoking in your home, have plenty of ashtrays laid out in prominent positions if you want to avoid having to deal with a mountain of butts in your plant pots the next day. If you don't allow smoking, put up a sign saying so.

Make up some signs pointing out where the bathroom is, where to leave coats and which rooms are off-limits. Ensure you have plenty of toilet paper, clean hand towels and soap in the bathroom.

Your rubbish bin will fill up quickly. Have a fresh bin liner in it and keep some spares in the bottom of the bin so you don't have to go searching around in cupboards when one gets filled up. Have a couple of large cardboard boxes at the ready somewhere out of the way, which you can fill up with bottles and other recyclables.

Finally, give your house a good clean! You may think that your guests won't notice that dubious-looking ring around your bath once they've had a few drinks, but they will.

**25 December
597**

England adopts the Julian calendar.

Why does Scrooge love Rudolph the Red-nosed Reindeer?

Because every buck is dear to him.

15

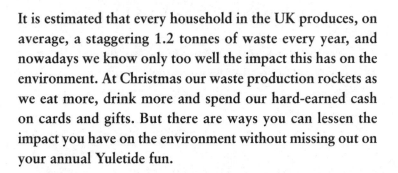

Having a Green Christmas

It is estimated that every household in the UK produces, on average, a staggering 1.2 tonnes of waste every year, and nowadays we know only too well the impact this has on the environment. At Christmas our waste production rockets as we eat more, drink more and spend our hard-earned cash on cards and gifts. But there are ways you can lessen the impact you have on the environment without missing out on your annual Yuletide fun.

Responsible gift-giving

Try to avoid buying presents that will only last for a week before breaking and those that use disposable parts. Check that any battery-powered gizmos you plan to give can use rechargeable batteries and, if necessary, purchase them separately to be included with your gift. Always look for greener alternatives, for example a coffee machine with a washable filter rather than a disposable one. Buy products made from recycled materials whenever possible – www.recycledproducts.org.uk has a huge list of such items. Always buy recycled and recyclable wrapping paper.

Vouchers and tokens are great environmentally friendly gifts, as well as allowing the recipient to choose something they actually want and will use.

16

'The one thing women don't want to find in their stockings on Christmas morning is their husband.'
JOAN RIVERS

Christmas cards

Around 1 billion Christmas cards end up in bins across the UK every year, which is a shocking waste considering that there are so many recycling schemes in place. Many local charity shops take in old Christmas cards and used stamps and the Woodland Trust (www.woodland-trust.org.uk/recycling) has set up card drops in high-street stores and supermarkets across the country. Do some research and find out what provisions have been made in your area.

Consider pruning your Christmas card list and sending fewer this year. You can always send an electronic card or email message instead. If you are sending cards, make sure that they are made from recycled materials – many charities sell these now. Keep and reuse old envelopes – many charities sell reuse labels. Keep a few of your more attractive Christmas cards to cut up and use as gift tags next year.

Trees and decorations

There are now many schemes in place to dispose of old trees in an environmentally friendly way, where they are composted to produce mulch – check with your local authority ahead of time to see if such a facility operates in your area. However, consider buying a tree with roots that can be replanted in your garden if you have the space, or kept in a pot for next year. Although fake trees are more often than not made from plastics, they should last for years and so are more or less environmentally sound.

Don't buy cheap, easily breakable decorations. Look for more expensive, durable versions and fill in the gaps by making your own out of scrap or edible materials (see pages 80–1 for some inspiration).

Food and drink

Avoid products that are packaged in a lot of unnecessary wrapping and buy goods that come in large bottles or cartons, rather than many smaller versions of the same product. Invest in some sturdy shopping bags or reuse old plastic ones when you go to the supermarket. Order any extra milk or juice from the milkman and return the bottles rather than buying plastic cartons.

Travel

If you are travelling over Christmas – or people are travelling to you – take responsibility for organizing car pools wherever possible. It'll minimize your impact on the environment as well as cutting out the usual parking nightmares.

' 'Twas the night before Christmas,
When all through the house
Not a creature was stirring, not
even a mouse;
The stockings were hung by the
chimney with care,
In hopes that St Nicholas soon
would be there.'

CLEMENT MOORE

The Origins of Christmas Traditions

SANTA CLAUS

The fat, jolly chap who delivers toys to all good children in just one night is known by many different names throughout the world, but in English-speaking countries he is most commonly referred to as Santa Claus or Father Christmas. The name Santa Claus comes from the Dutch *Sinterklaas* or *Sint Nicolaas*. St Nicholas was born in the third century in a part of Greece that is now Turkey. He devoted his life to helping the sick and needy, especially children, eventually being made Bishop of the city of Myra, which no longer exists. He was venerated throughout Europe and the date of 6 December, said to be the day on which he died, was dedicated to him. From the thirteenth century onwards it became customary for bishops to hand out small gifts to children who on this day had served the Church in St Nicholas's honour. In many countries this is still the day on which Christmas presents are exchanged.

St Nicholas later became associated with many early European folk tales concerning gift-giving, most notably one concerning a holy man and a demon, often referred to as Krampus. This terrifying figure was said to enter homes via chimneys and slaughter children or carry them away in a sack. The demon was finally trapped by a holy man, who forced him to make amends by delivering gifts to children.

In early seventeenth-century England, as a show of resistance to the Puritan disapproval of traditional Christmas festivities, the spirit of Christmas was personified in the shape of a fat, bearded man dressed in green fur-lined robes, thus giving rise to Father Christmas. He was also known as Sir Christmas or Lord Christmas, although he was not yet associated with gift-giving or children.

It was in North America that the modern image of Santa Claus was born, as colonists merged together the legends of St Nicholas and Father Christmas. In his *History of New York* (1809), Washington Irving translated *Sinterklaas* as 'Santa Claus'. This figure was given further shape by the classic poem 'A Visit from St Nicholas', better known today as 'The Night Before Christmas', which was first published in a New York newspaper in 1823. It was this poem that gave rise to the legend of Santa's reindeer.

Contrary to legend, it was not the Coca-Cola company that first introduced Santa's traditional red costume with their famous Christmas advertising campaigns of the 1930s. The modern depiction of Santa in red was started much earlier, in 1885, when a Christmas card designed by Boston printer Louis Prang went on sale.

True Christmas Stories: the Tale of the Festive Trousers

A long and most unusual feud between brothers-in-law Roy Collette and Larry Kunkel began in 1964 when Larry was given a pair of moleskin trousers by his mother. Larry didn't think much of the trousers and so he wrapped them up and gave them to Roy that Christmas. Unimpressed by his brother-in-law's thrifty re-gifting, Roy waited until the following Christmas and gave them back.

The annual trouser-exchange became a family tradition and for a few years the trousers were shunted back and forth in this manner until Roy decided to up the ante. That Christmas, Larry received the trousers as usual, except this time they were stuffed into a three-foot-long metal pole. From then on Ray and Larry would compete with each other every year to see who could come up with the most unusual method of wrapping. The aim was to try to remove the trousers without damaging them beyond repair, and they agreed that the contest would only end when the trousers were no more.

For twenty-five years, the trousers were subjected to some rather ingenious wrapping methods, which included stuffing them into a coffee can that was then soldered shut and placed inside a larger container filled with concrete, mounting them inside a double-glazed window with a twenty-year guarantee, putting them in a 600-pound safe

25 December
1066

William the
Conqueror is crowned
King of England.

What do you get if cross a snowman and a shark?

Frostbite.

that was then soldered shut, and locking them in the glove compartment of a written-off car, which was then crushed into a three-foot-square cube.

Amazingly, the trousers were extricated undamaged every time until their sad demise in 1989, when Larry had the idea of trying to encase them in 10,000 pounds of glass. Tragically, even these hardiest of trousers proved unable to withstand the stresses of molten glass and the contest – along with the trousers – finally came to an end.

'Mail your packages early so the post office can lose them in time for Christmas.'
JOHNNY CARSON

Present-wrapping Made Easy (1)

We would all like to see a pile of beautifully wrapped presents under the tree on Christmas morning, but lack of time and awkwardly shaped gifts often mean we end up with a higgledy-piggledy collection of lumpy packages covered in so much sticky tape that you need to spend a couple of hours with a sharp pair of scissors to get to the goodies within. If the thought of wrestling with wrapping paper fills you with despair, fret no more. Follow this handy guide to ensure your offerings are always perfectly presented.

Some top tips

❄ Don't leave your wrapping until the last minute; wrap your gifts as you buy them. If you're one of those people who make a mad dash to the shops with their lists just before closing time on Christmas Eve, turn to the sections on gift-buying and plan ahead this year.

❄ Boxes are easier to wrap than oddly shaped gifts, so put aside containers of various sizes throughout the year, fill them with layers of coloured tissue paper and pop in those hard-to-wrap presents.

❄ Gather everything you'll need to wrap your gifts before you start, including the paper (obviously), scissors, removable sticky tape, and perhaps a ruler – and make sure that you work on a large, flat surface.

24

❆ Using lots of small strips of sticky tape to secure your wrapping, rather than a few longer strips, will make your package look much neater. Cut some strips before you start wrapping and line them up along the edge of the surface you will be working on.

❆ Don't forget to remove any price tags before you wrap!

❆ Make sure you stick on a gift-tag or in some way label each present before you move on to the next, so you don't forget which is which.

How to wrap a box – beautifully

1. Although this may sound straightforward, it takes a little extra skill to get your gift looking special. Using the right amount of paper for your box is crucial, as messy wrapping is usually the result of using too much. The paper should be wide enough to cover about two-thirds of the height of the box. To get the right length, wrap a ribbon around the box to measure its girth, add two inches and use it as a guide when cutting out the paper. If you're not very handy with scissors, use a ruler and pencil to mark where you need to cut, or make folds in the paper.

2. Open up the paper out in front of you with the printed side facing down and lay the box on it, top down. Bring one lengthwise edge of paper up and tape it to the side of the box.

Make a hem along the opposite edge of the paper by folding it over about an inch, then bring it up so that it overlaps the first edge and tape it down. Make sure that the paper is very tightly wrapped around the box at this point.

3. Turn the box around so that one of the unsecured sides is facing you. Fold the right and left sides of paper inwards to form triangular flaps along the top and bottom, making sure that your creases are nice and tight. Bring the upper flap down, again making sure that your crease is very sharp, and tape it to the box. Bring the bottom flap up and secure it to the first flap.

4. Repeat step 3 on the other side and flip your perfectly wrapped gift the right way round to conceal as much unsightly tape as possible.

How to wrap a tube or cylinder

The easiest way to wrap presents that are cylindrical is to use tissue paper and ribbon to form a sort of cracker. You don't need to worry about too much paper in this case – leave some excess paper on each side of the tube, and enough to wrap around the tube a couple of times so that the packaging doesn't show through.

1. Lay the tissue or wrapping paper in front of you, printed side down, and place the tube in the centre but a few inches above one of the edges.

2. Bring the edge of the tissue paper up and tape it to the tube. Then simply roll the tube along the rest of the paper, making sure that it is tightly wrapped. Tape down the other edge.

3. Twist both the open ends around, sealing the gift inside and forming a cracker shape, and secure the ribbon by tying it in knots over the twists. If you pull the ends of the ribbon over the blunt edges of the scissor blades the ribbon will curl and look more decorative.

How to wrap a wine bottle

Bottles of bubbly are always appreciated at Christmas but they can be tricky to wrap. Rather than just presenting them in a gift bag, use some coloured or printed cellophane to wrap them.

25 December
1223

St Francis of Assisi assembles the first Nativity scene in Greccio, Italy.

Simply place the bottle in the centre of a piece of cellophane and bring the sides up around it, securing the covering at the top with some ribbon tied around the neck of the bottle. The present will look much better if it's not covered in sticky tape.

Some Unusual Places to Hide Presents from Prying Kids

❄ Up your jumper

❄ In the oven

❄ Up the chimney (though this may provide an authentic present-arriving-from-Santa scenario on Christmas morning)

❄ In the fruit bowl (most kids never go near one)

❄ Underneath the cat

❄ Inside the turkey

❄ Under the patio

❄ On top of the tree

❄ On the mantelpiece

❄ Behind your back

The Origins of Christmas Traditions

CHRISTMAS CARDS

Although religiously-themed prints made by wood engravers date back to the Middle Ages, the Christmas card is a relatively recent tradition. The widespread exchange of home-made Christmas cards began in Britain in 1840, with the introduction of the first postal service, the Penny Post. The man who played a key role in setting up the Penny Post, Sir Henry Cole, commissioned London artist John Calcott Horsley to produce the first commercially printed Christmas card in 1843. One thousand copies of the card, which depicted a family party and scenes of the poor being clothed and fed, with the inscription 'A merry Christmas and a happy New Year to you', were placed on sale. The tradition took off over the next few years as printing methods improved, and by 1860 large numbers were being produced.

Famous People Born on Christmas Day

Humphrey Bogart, actor (1899)

Conrad Hilton, hotelier (1887)

Annie Lennox, singer (1954)

Kenny Everett, comedian (1944)

Pius VI, pope (1717)

Tony Martin, actor and singer (1912)

Bernhard Jr, Prince of the Netherlands (1969)

Howard Hughes, businessman, film director and aviator (1905)

Sissy Spacek, actress (1949)

Anwar al-Sadat, Egyptian President and Nobel Peace Prize-winner (1918)

Dido, singer (1971)

Christmas Spirits

If the stress of last-minute shopping, frantic wrapping, endless To Do lists and cooking a delicious meal for fifty is getting you down, try one or two of these seasonal pick-me-ups. After all, 'tis the season to be jolly!

Eggnog (Serves 8 to 10)

You can replace the rum and brandy with whisky for a different flavour if you want. It's best to prepare the eggnog just before serving as the mixture will separate after a while.

6 large eggs	850 ml (1½ pints) milk
170 g (6 oz) sugar	850 ml (1½ pints) cream
110 ml (4 fl. oz) rum	110 g (4 oz) icing sugar
340 ml (12 fl. oz) brandy	Nutmeg, finely grated

1. Carefully separate the eggs into two large bowls. Start to beat the yolks, then add the sugar, bit by bit, beating all the time until the mixture is smooth and pale. Slowly pour in the rum and brandy and mix thoroughly, then beat in the milk and half the cream. Set aside.

2. Whisk the egg whites until they are stiff and gently fold them into the yolk mixture. In another bowl, whip the remaining cream with the icing sugar until it has a thick consistency.

3. Pour the egg-yolk mixture into punch glasses and top with the whipped cream and a sprinkling of grated nutmeg.

Mulled wine (Serves 4 to 6)

Christmas just isn't the same without it.

1 bottle full-bodied red wine	8 cloves
1 glass port or sherry	2 oranges, sliced
1 cinnamon stick	1 lemon, sliced
1 bay leaf	6 tsp caster sugar
6 juniper berries	

Pour the wine into a large saucepan and throw in all the other ingredients. Heat very gently, stirring all the time, until the sugar is dissolved. Do not allow the wine to boil. Strain through a sieve and ladle into heatproof glasses.

25 December 1683

Spain declares war on France.

25 December 1688

England's King James II escapes to France.

'At Christmas play and make good cheer, for Christmas comes but once a year.'
THOMAS TUSSER

Champagne cocktail with ginger (Serves 1)

Everybody's got a few bottles of bubbly lying around at Christmas. The spiciness of the ginger makes this a good winter alternative to the classic Bellini.

2 thin slices of ginger
1 measure vodka
Champagne

Crush the slices of ginger slightly to release the full flavour and place in a cocktail shaker. Add ice and the vodka and shake well. Strain the mixture into a flute and top with champagne.

Snowball (Serves 1)

As its name suggests, this is the perfect cocktail for the festive season. The creaminess of the Advocaat is cut by the tang of the lemon and lime, making it a good alternative to the rather rich eggnog.

2 measures Advocaat
Lime cordial
Lemonade

Pour the Advocaat into a cocktail shaker and add just a dash of lime cordial. Shake well, pour into a highball glass filled with ice and top with lemonade.

Hot toddy (Serves 1)

The ultimate winter reviver and guaranteed to warm you up on those cold winter evenings.

2 measures whisky	1 tsp honey
25 ml lemon juice, freshly squeezed	1 lemon slice
75 ml hot water	1 cinnamon stick

Pour the whisky into a heatproof glass, add the lemon juice and top with hot water. Stir in the honey and garnish with the lemon slice and cinnamon stick before serving.

Santa's Rules

It seems that even Santa needs some basic rules by which to conduct himself. Jenny Zinc, an employee for a US temping agency that has trained and supplied Santas to department stores for over thirty years, sums up the most important tenets of Santa etiquette as follows:

'Santa is even-tempered.

Santa does not hit children over the head who kick him.

Santa uses the term "folks" rather than "Mommy" and "Daddy" because of all the broken homes.

Santa does not have a three-martini lunch.

Santa does not borrow money from store employees.

Santa wears a good deodorant.'

The Origins of Christmas Traditions

STOCKINGS

The practice of hanging up stockings can be traced back to pre-Christian times. Germanic folklore tells of the god Odin's annual Yuletime hunting party. Children would leave out their shoes filled with straw or sugar for Odin's flying horse, and Odin would reward them by leaving small gifts in exchange. Later on, the practice was linked with St Nicholas. The story goes that a nobleman with three daughters had fallen on hard times and was unable to give his daughters dowries so that they could be married. St Nicholas wanted to help but also remain anonymous, so he threw some gold coins down the chimney, where they landed in the girls' stockings that had been hung by the fire to dry.

Alternative Uses for Brussels Sprouts

For many, the Brussels Sprout is a thing of beauty and joy, a delicious and nutritious legume, without which Christmas dinner just wouldn't be the same. For others, it is Satan's vegetative representative on earth. If you are of the latter persuasion and would go to any lengths not to have to actually eat one, here are some alternative uses:

❄ Dip a handful in melted chocolate and place them in an empty box of chocolates, ready to be presented to your least favourite relative.

❄ No white Christmas this year? Never mind. Have a mock snowball fight using the little green devils instead. You'll be smelling of sprout for weeks.

❄ Thread a dozen or so together and make a wonderful alternative to the classic pearl necklace.

❄ Leave a plate out for Santa instead of the usual mince pie – he could do with shedding a few pounds. Be prepared for some disappointment when it comes to opening your presents though.

❄ Draw the numbers 1 to 49 on them with a magic marker and place them in the tumble dryer for a novel way to pick your lottery numbers.

'Roses are
reddish
Violets are bluish
If it weren't for
Christmas
We'd all be Jewish.'
BENNY HILL

❉ Surreptitiously feed them to your dog while no one is looking. The subsequent digestive results will get rid of any unwanted house guests in no time at all.

❉ Teach yourself how to juggle with them.

❉ Sprinkle them with glitter and dangle them from the Christmas tree – they make great decorations. For a couple of days, at least.

What do angry mice send to each other at Christmas?

Cross-mouse cards.

25 December
1717

Thousands lose
their lives as floods
ravage Dutch coastal
provinces.

Dear   [name of stingy relative],

Thank you so much for your very generous cheque. It's great that you refuse to be pressured by the ridiculously stringent gift-giving rules of etiquette.

Despite our intimate family connection, I would hate for you to put yourself to the trouble of hunting down and purchasing a more personal gift. I regret that I was unable not to 'spend it all at once', as by the time I had purchased this thank-you card, there was only just enough money left for the bus fare home.

Yours sincerely,

Christmas Lunch

Preparing Christmas lunch is a bit like planning a military operation. If you're going for the traditional turkey with all the trimmings, you need to make sure you're properly organized. The trick is to plan ahead as much as possible so that you're not rushing around trying to do a hundred things at once at the last minute. Prepare as much as you can before Christmas morning and draw up a detailed timetable to remind you when you should be doing what. Of course, menus will vary and cooking times will depend on the quantities you are serving, but below is a handy timetable that can be used as a rough guide to help make Christmas Day as stress-free as possible.

Well ahead of time

If you're making a Christmas pudding, you should prepare it at least a month, preferably more, before Christmas Day, to allow all the flavours to develop.

The week before

If you're making your own sauces, now is the time to start doing so. Cranberry sauce is easy to prepare and will keep for a year if you store it in properly sterilized jars. Make a large batch and keep some aside for next year. Bread sauce also freezes well.

❄ If you like to serve some stuffing separately, prepare and cook it now, in a freezer-proof oven dish, and freeze.

❄ Make your mince pies and store them in an airtight container, ready to be reheated on Christmas Day.

❄ Brandy butter can be quickly whipped up and will keep for a long time in the fridge.

'I stopped believing in Santa Claus when I was six. Mother took me to see him in a department store and he asked for my autograph.'

SHIRLEY TEMPLE

Two days before

❄ If you're cooking a frozen turkey, remove it from the freezer now, so that there is no last-minute panic. Being faced with a half-defrosted turkey floating in the bath is not a great start to Christmas morning. When it is fully defrosted, keep it in the fridge.

Christmas Eve

❄ Remove the bread sauce and cooked stuffing from the freezer to defrost overnight.

❄ Prepare the sprouts, so that they are ready for boiling the next day.

❄ If you're stuffing the turkey, prepare the raw mixture and leave in the fridge overnight.

❄ Remove the giblets from the turkey and prepare the stock for the gravy. Store it in an airtight container in the fridge overnight.

❄ Sharpen your preparation and carving knives.

❄ Lay the table.

❄ Last thing at night, remove the turkey from the fridge and leave it out, covered, so that it can come up to room temperature.

Christmas Day

The following timetable is for a 14 lb (6.5 kg) turkey. If your turkey is a different size adjust the timings as necessary.

7.45 a.m. Preheat the oven to 220°C/425°F /Gas mark 7. Get some butter out of the fridge and give it a quick blast in the microwave to soften it. Stuff the turkey, rub it all over with butter, season it and lay some streaky bacon over the breast. Wrap the turkey in foil.

8.15 a.m. Put the turkey in the oven. Peel your potatoes and parsnips and place them in cold water until you are ready to cook them.

9.00 a.m. Turn the oven temperature down to 170°C/325°F/ Gas mark 3. Remove the brandy butter from the fridge. Wrap the chipolatas in bacon and place on a baking tray.

11.00 a.m. Put the Christmas pudding on to steam. Don't forget to check the water level occasionally.

12.30 p.m. Turn the oven temperature up to 200°C/400°F/ Gas mark 6. Remove the turkey from the oven, take it out of its foil and remove the bacon from the breasts. Baste well and return to the oven. Keep basting regularly. If you are serving the separate, pre-cooked stuffing, cover the oven dish with foil and place it at the bottom of the oven.

12.45 p.m. Place some oil or fat in a roasting tray and put in the oven. Parboil the potatoes for ten minutes, then drain them and give them a good shake in the dry pan.

1.00 p.m. Transfer the potatoes to the roasting dish and return to the oven. Add some oil to another roasting tray and place in the oven.

1.15 p.m. Check the turkey is cooked through by inserting a skewer into the thickest part of the thigh. If the juices run clear, it's done, if they are pinkish, cook it for a little longer. Once it is cooked through, remove from the oven, put onto a warm plate and cover with foil. Turn the oven temperature up to 230°C/450°F/Gas mark 8. Remove the potatoes and drain off the fat, then place them on the highest shelf of the oven. Put the parsnips in the second roasting tray and return to the middle shelf of the oven. Place the chipolatas at the bottom of the oven. Heat up your pre-prepared stock and use it to make your gravy. Check the seasoning and place it to one side.

1.45 p.m. Put the sprouts on to boil. Reheat your gravy and gently warm through any additional sauces. From now on keep a close eye on your sauces and vegetables and transfer them to serving dishes as they become ready.

2.00 p.m. Lunch is served! Before you sit down to eat, turn down the oven to a very low heat and put in the mince pies to warm up.

44

A Very Veggie Christmas

Catering for vegetarian guests or family members doesn't have to be a chore. With a bit of thought and planning ahead you can easily accommodate them without adding too much to your workload, and they'll appreciate your forethought. Consider the following points:

❄ Talk to your veggie guest before you plan your vegetarian menu. Some vegetarians love meat substitutes; others can't stand the taste and texture of anything resembling meat. Make sure you ask whether they are vegetarian or vegan (vegans eschew dairy products and eggs as well as meat).

❄ Many foods that don't contain meat may still contain animal products. Some desserts contain gelatine, and animal rennet is often used in cheese, for example. Look for the 'V' sign on food packaging if you are unsure whether something is suitable.

25 December 1741

Astronomer Anders Celsius introduces the Centigrade temperature scale.

❄ Make your mince pies and Christmas pudding with vegetable suet or ensure they have vegetarian labels if you are buying them pre-made.

❄ Provide vegetarian wine! Wine is often clarified with animal products.

❄ You don't have to cook an entirely separate meal. Your vegetarian guests will be more than happy to share your vegetable side dishes. Just make sure you keep all your vegetables well away from any meat and cook them in vegetable fat. Choose a meat-free stuffing that everyone will enjoy.

❄ Health food stores and some supermarkets stock excellent ready-made vegetarian options, so there's no need to slave away in the kitchen any more than you already are. If you do want to go to the trouble of cooking something yourself, opt for something more original than the traditional offering of nut roast, such as a chestnut bourguignon pie. Here's the recipe!

'Heap on
more wood!
The wind is chill;
But let it whistle as it
will, We'll keep our
Christmas merry still.'
SIR WALTER SCOTT

Chestnut bourguignon pie (Serves 4 to 6)

The day before making this delicious pie, soak the chestnuts in cold water for about 6 to 8 hours, then drain.

125 g (4½ oz) dried chestnuts	125 g (4½ oz) chestnut mushrooms
2 bay leaves	125 g (4½ oz) button mushrooms
1 sprig rosemary	2 tsp Dijon mustard
210 ml (7½ fl. oz)	2 tbsp soy sauce
Vegetarian red wine	1 tbsp parsley, finely chopped
300 ml (10½ fl. oz) vegetable stock	Salt and freshly ground black pepper,
8 shallots, peeled	to taste
25 g (1 oz) butter	225 g (8 oz) vegetarian puff pastry

1. Place the chestnuts, bay leaves and rosemary in a saucepan along with the vegetable stock and 150 ml (5 fl. oz) of the red wine. Gently simmer for about an hour, or until the chestnuts are tender. Drain the chestnuts, reserving the liquid.

2. Preheat the oven to 200°C/400°F/Gas mark 6.

3. Fry the shallots in the butter until slightly browned, then add the mushrooms and sauté for 5 minutes. Add the chestnuts, the remaining red wine and enough of the reserved liquid to cover, and stir in the mustard, soy sauce and parsley. Bring to the boil and simmer for 30 minutes. Season to taste.

4. Put the mixture in a pie dish. Roll out the pastry on a floured surface, place over the top of the dish and trim around the edges. Bake for 20 minutes, until golden brown.

47

Top Ten Christmas Movies (1)

Christmas is a time for family, friends, counting our blessings and . . . television. Despite our best efforts to bully or cajole our loved ones into turning off the box and playing yet another game of charades, sometimes it's best just to give in. So turn the lights down low, put another log on the fire and surrender to the joys of a classic Christmas movie.

It's a Wonderful Life (1946)

Can there possibly be a person on the planet who hasn't seen this film? Despite its popularity today, *It's a Wonderful Life* was a box-office flop when it was released and only gained classic status in the 70s, when it was repeatedly aired on TV during the holiday season.

Surprisingly gritty and dark for a Christmas movie, *It's a Wonderful Life* tells the story of small-town do-gooder George Bailey (James Stewart), who on Christmas Eve finds himself on the brink of bankruptcy and facing a spell in prison due to the machinations of town villain Mr Potter (Lionel Barrymore). George is saved from a suicide attempt by wingless guardian angel Clarence Oddbody (Henry Travers). Clarence shows George how much worse off the town would have been without his numerous good deeds, thus restoring George's faith in himself and earning Clarence his wings.

CLARENCE: *Strange, isn't it? Each man's life touches so many other lives. When he isn't around he leaves an awful hole, doesn't he?*

A Christmas Carol/Scrooge (1951)

Charles Dickens's classic Christmas tale has had many film incarnations, but the 1951 version is arguably the best, mainly because of Alastair Sim's brilliant performance in the title role. The plot is faithful to Dickens's story. Ebenezer Scrooge is a bitter old man obsessed with money and scornful of charity. On Christmas Eve he is visited by four spirits sent to teach him the error of his ways and deliver a dire warning of what might lie ahead for him if he does not redeem himself. By Christmas morning he is a changed man and the story ends on a satisfyingly Christmassy note of goodwill to all men.

EBENEZER: *I am standing in the presence of the Spirit of Christmas Yet To Come? And you're going to show me the shadows of things that have not yet happened but will happen? Spirit of the Future, I fear you more than any spectre I have met tonight! But even in my fear, I must say that I am too old! I cannot change! I cannot! It's not that I'm impenitent, it's just . . . Wouldn't it be better if I just went home to bed?*

Miracle on 34th Street (1947)

Kris Kringle (Edmund Gwenn), hired by Doris Walker (Maureen O'Hara) of Macy's department store in New York to replace their drunken store Santa, proves to be a wild success, inspiring all around him with his honesty and kindness. There's just one snag though: Kringle believes he is the real Santa. Following a showdown with Macy's horrible in-store psychologist, Kringle is declared insane and incarcerated. Doris's lawyer friend Fred Gailey (John Payne) comes to the rescue by taking on his case and endeavours to prove in court that Kringle is indeed the real Father Christmas. A heartwarming tale made extra-special by Gwenn's Oscar-winning performance.

MEMORABLE QUOTE

FRED GAILEY: *Faith is believing when common sense tells you not to. Don't you see? It's not just Kris that's on trial, it's everything he stands for. It's kindness and joy and love and all the other intangibles.*

25 December
1758

Halley's Comet is first sighted by German astronomer Johann Georg Palitzsch.

Rudolph the Red-Nosed Reindeer (1964)

This animated Rankin/Bass film breathed new life into one of Christmas's most enduring characters. It tells the tale of Santa's ninth reindeer, Rudolph, shunned by his peers because of his shiny red nose. Rudolph teams up with fellow misfit Hermey, an elf who wants to be a dentist, and they leave the North Pole to find a place where they can belong. Along with new friend Yukon Cornelius, they take on the Abominable Snowmonster and stumble upon an island populated with misshapen toys. The inevitable happy ending sees Rudolph welcomed back to the fold and putting his proboscis to good use guiding Santa's sleigh through the fog. The stop-motion animation may be very different to today's computer-generated offerings, but it has immense charm. One for all the family.

MEMORABLE QUOTE

YUKON CORNELIUS: *Fog's as thick as peanut butter.*
HERMEY: *You mean pea soup.*
YUKON CORNELIUS: *You eat what you like and I'll eat what I like.*

What if there had been three Wise Women instead of three Wise Men?

They would have asked for directions, arrived on time, helped deliver the baby, cleaned the stable and brought practical gifts.

Scrooged (1988)

Another version of Dickens's Christmas classic, this time set in the present and starring Bill Murray at his cynical best. Frank Cross is a successful but mean-spirited and friendless TV producer given the task of staging a live broadcast of *A Christmas Carol*. Life begins to imitate art when he is visited by four spirits and . . . well, you know the rest. Murray's superb performance, some sharp dialogue and a sentimental ending make this a hugely enjoyable spin on an old tale.

MEMORABLE QUOTE

JAMES CROSS: *You know what they say about people who treat other people bad on the way up?*

FRANK CROSS: *Yeah, you get to treat 'em bad on the way back down too. It's great, you get two chances to rough 'em up.*

'It was always said of him, that he knew how to keep Christmas well, if any man alive possessed the knowledge. May that be truly said of us, and all of us! And so, as Tiny Tim observed, God Bless Us, Every One!'

CHARLES DICKENS

The Twelve Days of Christmas

A partridge in a pear tree
Two turtle doves
Three French hens
Four calling birds
Five gold rings
Six geese a-laying
Seven swans a-swimming
Eight maids a-milking
Nine ladies dancing
Ten lords a-leaping
Eleven pipers piping
Twelve drummers drumming

53

All I Want for Christmas . . .

Christmas is a time for peace on earth and goodwill to all men. It is also a time for presents. Whatever you may feel about the commercialization of Christmas, unless you are the modern reincarnation of Ebenezer Scrooge you most probably have to tackle each year the task of planning and budgeting for the annual exchange of gifts. If you don't put sufficient care and thought into the process, it is all too easy to end up in a frenzy of last-minute impulse-purchasing, which inevitably means hugely overspending on an assortment of odds and ends that you are not sure anybody will like. This is not to say that you should rush out and buy all your gifts in the January sales, though. Just a bit of forward planning and some creative thinking will ensure your popularity this Christmas.

Planning ahead

Lists

The good old list is your friend; use him well. Keep a notebook in a drawer somewhere where you can jot down gift ideas throughout the year. Next time Auntie Mabel mentions that she's smashed another plate from her precious dinner-service set, make a note of it. Come Christmas or her birthday you can track down a replacement and voila! Instant Brownie points for showing that you were listening and cared enough to remember.

Budgets

Settle on a budget that is within your means and stick to it. If you don't keep track of what you are spending you'll end up crying over your post-Christmas bank statement. Successful gift-giving does not mean splashing out on expensive designer goods that will inevitably end up stashed away in the back of a cupboard. It's usually the inexpensive, thoughtful presents that are the most cherished. A new edition of a favourite childhood book is worth ten stainless-steel espresso machines that will never be used. Have a bit of extra cash set aside as a contingency. That way, if you spot the perfect present for that difficult-to-buy-for teenager who already has every gadget known to man, but it costs a bit more than you were planning to spend, you can go ahead and get it without feeling guilty about overspending or having to cut back elsewhere.

Avoiding the High Street

For the shopaholics among us, there's much pleasure to be had in the annual pilgrimage to the High Street with its Christmas lights and window displays. For those who dread the crush and the queues, there are, thankfully, alternatives.

Catalogues

Most of the major stores produce Christmas catalogues that you can send off for or pick up next time you are in town. The convenience of being able to shop from home is great, but there are a few things you should watch out for:

❄ Don't be tempted to impulse-buy. Have a clear idea in your head of what you are looking for and how much you want to spend before you start flicking through those pages.

❄ Do thoroughly read the payment terms on store cards before you make an order, particularly the interest rates, which are most often very high indeed. Always pay off your purchases in full if you can afford it (and you should be able to, if you are sticking to your carefully planned budget).

❄ Do check the terms of delivery to make sure you order your goods on time and that there is someone at home to accept the delivery.

❄ Do check the returns policy, in case the goods are not up to scratch.

The Internet

The great thing about shopping on the Web, apart from the convenience, is that you can buy pretty much anything under the sun, and many things that you won't be able to find in shops. All the dos and don'ts listed above apply to Internet shopping as well, but there are a few other things to consider.

Security is an important issue. Do your homework before you whip out your credit card and thoroughly research the company you want to buy from. There are websites, such as shopsafe.co.uk, that list only secure shopping sites, and which give them a rating based on security, customer service, range of goods and price. Always read the site's security policy. Many sites offer an alternative telephone payment service. Use this if you are nervous about putting your account details online. Always print out copies of your order details and keep them in a safe place.

Internet auction sites like eBay are incredibly popular and there are fantastic bargains to be had. Bear in mind, though, that in most cases you will be buying from individuals rather than companies and so there is more chance of late delivery (or no delivery) and of goods being not as described. Although these sites offer various means of redress if you are not happy with the service you receive, it will inevitably take time to sort out any problems, so order well ahead of time. Only buy from sellers with a good track record and positive customer feedback. Carefully read the seller's description of the goods before you make a bid and print a copy for your records. Save and print out any emails exchanged. Never do deals with sellers outside of the site – some fraudsters will email people who have lost out on an auction with offers of similar goods. If you receive an email like this, do not reply to it – pass it on to the auction site.

25 December 1868

President Andrew Johnson grants unconditional pardon to everyone involved in the Southern rebellion against the United States.

To re-gift or not to re-gift?

Although some people have got re-gifting down to a fine art (see page 22 for an example of truly imaginative re-gifting), the pitfalls are such that it is generally best avoided. The only time it is acceptable is if the gift is a genuinely good one, just not quite to your taste or you already have a similar item. If you think so little of someone that you are happy to give them the hideous Donald Duck socks your visually impaired Uncle Albert gave you last year, then it's best to forgo a gift altogether and just send a friendly card. If you can't bear to throw your unwanted presents away, donate them to a charity shop. Someone out there might like them, it's just unlikely that it will be the person you're planning on giving them to.

If you must re-gift, always remember the golden rule: keep track of who gave you what!

Grab bags

If you're hosting or attending a large gathering of family and friends, instead of buying a gift for each and every person, why not suggest a 'grab-bag' exchange? Each person spends a pre-agreed amount on just one gift. All the gifts are wrapped and placed into a large sack, and everyone picks a number out of a hat. 'Number one' picks out a parcel and opens it in front of everyone else, then 'number two' has a turn, and so on. Once everyone has a present, the exchanging begins. Number one has first choice to swap his or her gift with someone else's, then everyone else has a go in order, with the person who picked the final number having the last say.

The Alternative Christmas Message

George V gave the first Royal Christmas Message in 1932 and since then it has become a national institution, as much a part of Christmas Day as indigestion and too much sherry. In 1993, Channel 4 invited Quentin Crisp to deliver an alternative message and since then a string of contemporary and often controversial figures have been invited to share their thoughts with the nation on the events of the year.

1993	Quentin Crisp
1994	Reverend Jesse Jackson
1995	Brigitte Bardot
1996	Rory Bremner (as Diana, Princess of Wales)
1997	Belfast schoolgirl Margaret Gibney (on peace in Northern Ireland)
1998	The parents of race-killing victim Stephen Lawrence, Neville and Doreen Lawrence
1999	Ali G
2000	Helen Jeffries, the mother of CJD victim Zoe Jeffries
2001	9/11 survivor Genelle Guzman
2002	Sharon Osbourne
2003	'Stars' of reality show *Wife Swap*, Barry and Michelle Seabourn
2004	Marge Simpson
2005	Jamie Oliver
2006	Khadijah, a veiled Muslim woman

THE CHRISTMAS TREE

The Christmas tree tradition most likely has its origins in pagan times, when evergreens were symbolic of new life and hope for the coming year.

The fir tree, however, also has a place in early Christianity. St Boniface was born in England in 675 and dedicated his life to converting the pagans. In 719 he was sent to Germany by Pope Gregory II to continue his missionary work. It is said that at Geismar he came across a group of pagans worshipping an oak tree, which was associated with the god Thor, and he cut it down in a fit of anger. In its place sprung a fir tree and Boniface declared that this was to be the new Christian symbol.

But it was not until much later that the Christmas tree as we know it came to be. A plaque in the town square in Riga, Latvia declares that the first 'New Year's tree' was to be found there in 1510. At around the same time, it is said that the German theologian Martin Luther was walking in an evergreen forest at night and was so struck by the beauty of the stars shining through the branches that he brought a tree home and decorated it with candles.

The first record of a decorated fir tree associated with Christmas time comes from Bremen in Germany in 1570, where a fir tree was brought into the guild house and decorated with fruit and nuts, which were then given to the local children on Christmas Day.

Many people believe that it was Queen Victoria's consort Prince Albert who introduced the Christmas tree tradition, already widespread in his native Germany, to Britain, but records dating from 1800 show that the Queen's grandmother, Charlotte, also a German, brought the custom to King George III's court. It was certainly during Victoria's reign, however, that the Christmas tree became popular outside of the royal family in Britain, with Albert donating Christmas trees to barracks and schools, and illustrations of the royal family with their tree appearing in magazines.

Choosing the
Right Christmas Tree

The Christmas tree has had an essential role in Yuletide celebrations for hundreds of years. These days there are so many options available that choosing a tree can be confusing. Whether you prefer the delicious scent of a traditional fir, the convenience of an artificial tree or want to try something a little bit different, this handy guide will help you make that all-important decision.

Traditional trees

Evergreen conifers are the trees traditionally associated with Christmas and there are many varieties available to choose from. Some of the most popular to be found for sale in Europe are listed below, along with some pros and cons to consider when making your decision:

Norwegian Spruce: Generally among the cheapest. Has an attractive bushy shape, but the needles are prickly and sparse, and tend to shed earlier than other varieties. Buy it as near to Christmas as possible and keep it well-watered.

Noble Fir: Has a lovely deep-green colour and a full, bushy shape. There's plenty of space between the branches and the needles are not too prickly, making it easy to decorate.

Nordman Fir: A very popular choice due to the fact that its needles don't shed easily and its branches are sturdy enough to hold many ornaments. It is among the most expensive, though, as it is slow to grow.

Blue Spruce: Has beautiful silver-blue foliage and is one of the most aromatic trees. It retains its needles quite well, but they are very sharp, so watch you don't step on them.

Scots Pine: Has a very attractive, full shape. Its long, prickly needles can make it tricky to decorate, but it retains them extremely well. Its branches are not very sturdy, so avoid heavy ornaments.

25 December 1901

The Boers defeat the British at Tweefontein.

Why does Father Christmas cry a lot?

Because he gets a little santamental.

Caring for your tree

POTTED TREES

Live, potted trees will last much longer and are very easy to care for: just make sure you keep the compost moist at all times, as you would with any other household plant. If you have the outdoor space available, do consider planting your tree outside after the Christmas period. If you're planning to do this, here are some things to bear in mind:

❄ Carefully research the type of tree that will suit the space you have available and the environmental conditions in your area.

❄ Don't keep your tree indoors for too long – five to seven days is the maximum – and keep it away from radiators and other sources of heat.

❄ Keep your tree outside in its pot for a month before you plant it, so that it can acclimatize.

❄ Dig a hole that is as deep as the measurement from the bottom of the root ball to the soil level and double the width of the root ball.

❄ When you are ready to plant, loosen up the outside roots a bit. Keep the soil around the tree weed-free and well-watered. When the ground has frozen over, cover it with mulch.

'Santa is very jolly because he knows where all the bad girls live.'

DENNIS MILLER

CUT TREES

❄ Invest in a good stand that can be filled with water and reused every year. Always fill the stand with water, not soil or sand, and top it up every day.

❄ Before you bring your tree indoors, cut about an inch off the trunk – this will help the tree to take up water – and give it a shake to get rid of any loose needles.

❄ Keep the tree away from any sources of heat.

❄ When Christmas is over, research any tree-recycling schemes that might be available in your area.

Alternative live trees

Other types of evergreen trees that can be grown and kept in pots make for attractive, original and environmentally friendly alternatives to the traditional tree. Consider bay trees, holly trees and citrus trees, and tailor your ornamentation accordingly. Bay trees, for example, look wonderful when decorated with miniature baubles. An indoor lemon tree can be adorned with bows of yellow ribbon, with a matching length of ribbon wound around the trunk.

What's the difference between the ordinary alphabet and the Christmas alphabet?

The Christmas alphabet has no L.

Artificial trees

Many people turn their noses up at the idea of an artificial tree, but in these environmentally conscious times, they are becoming more and more popular. The trees available nowadays are a far cry from the lurid, plastic creations of the past. You are not limited to imitation firs: how about a beautiful twig tree for a natural look, or a modern, minimalist metal tree? There's something out there to suit every budget, but consider splashing out a little to ensure a quality tree. You'll be using it year after year, after all, so you'll be saving money in the end. And be sure to investigate suitable recycling options when you decide that its best Christmases are behind it.

**What did Santa say to Mrs Claus
when he looked out the window?**

'Looks like rain, dear.'

'I heard the bells on Christmas Day;
Their old familiar carols play,
And wild and sweet the words repeat
Of peace on earth, goodwill to men!'
HENRY WADSWORTH LONGFELLOW

Dear [name of relative with no taste],

I wish you had been here to witness the gasps of awe when I unwrapped the delightful glow-in-the-dark Jesus statue/novelty fake-fur lampshade/pink ceramic kitten. Your gift was the cause of much joy and laughter in our household, and for that I thank you.

We were terrified that your precious gift might be inadvertently damaged, so we found it a safe home in a dark corner of the cellar, where it will remain for ever.

Yours sincerely,

Christmas Around the World

If you think the idea of a fat old man and a bunch of elves delivering presents to all the children in the world in just one night is wacky, you'll be amazed at some of the weird and wonderful ways our neighbours celebrate the festive season.

Greece

The Greeks don't tend to go in for Christmas trees. Instead many homes display a wooden bowl filled with water, over which is suspended a sprig of basil wrapped around a wooden cross. Every day throughout the twelve days of Christmas, a household member will dip the cross in holy water and sprinkle it around the house. This is thought to keep away the *Killantzaroi*, mischievous goblins who enter homes via the chimney during this time and cause mayhem. Give me Santa any day.

Greenland

If you're sick of the same old turkey dinner year after year, why not try the delicious-sounding *kiviak*, the traditional Christmas fare of Greenland? *Kiviak* is raw auk meat that has been wrapped in sealskin and buried for several months, until it is nicely decomposed and suitably whiffy. Or how about a tasty piece of *mattak* – whale skin with blubber attached? Yummy!

Guatemala

In the run-up to Christmas, Guatemalans believe that the devil runs riot and they 'celebrate' this by dressing up in suitably demonic style and chasing children through the streets. This culminates in *La Quema del Diablo*, 'the Burning of the Devil', on 7 December, when households gather together unwanted items and place them outside where they are set on fire in an attempt to drive the devil away. I suppose it's one way to get rid of the clutter you've accumulated throughout the year.

Iceland

You would be forgiven for thinking that the children of Iceland are lucky, for they have not one but thirteen Santas, who enter homes one by one on each of the thirteen days leading up to Christmas. But as these *Jolasveinar*, or 'Christmas Lads', are actually hideous trolls with names like 'Meat Hook' and 'Door Slammer', how lucky are they really?

25 December
1914

The Christmas Day truce occurs between British and German troops on the Western Front.

Mexico

The residents of Oaxaca, Mexico have a truly unique Christmas celebration: the *Noche de Rabanos* – 'Night of the Radishes' – celebrated on 23 December and commemorating the introduction of the radish by Spanish colonists in the mid-nineteenth century. The radishes grown in the region are enormous, measuring up to two feet in length and weighing up to ten pounds, and every year a contest is held to see who can carve them into the most elaborate Nativity figurines or scenes. All hail the mighty radish!

Poland

In Poland, Christmas Eve is traditionally a night when magic abounds. It is said that people gain fortune-telling powers and animals are able to speak in human voices. Many of these old traditions are still practised in the form of general Christmas fun and games. For example, unmarried girls are blindfolded on the way to Midnight Mass and try to touch a fence picket. If it is smooth and straight, they will find a good husband; if it is crooked, they will attract a less than ideal spouse.

Spain

From the Catalan region of Spain comes what is undoubtedly the strangest of Christmas figures – the *Caganer*, literally translated as 'the defecator'. The figure is portrayed squatting, with its trousers round its ankles – the rest I'll leave to your imagination. The origins of the *Caganer* are unclear, but is has been around since the seventeenth century and is an essential, if incongruous, part of any Catalonian Nativity scene. In fact, there was a public outcry in 2005, when the Barcelona city council commissioned a Nativity scene that did not include a *Caganer*.

Ukraine

If you're an arachnophobe you will want to steer well clear of the Ukraine at Christmas, as the eight-legged horrors are positively encouraged into homes around the country at this time of year. The practice comes from an old folk tale about a poor family who were visited by magic spiders one Christmas who turned all the webs in the house into silver and gold.

What do you call someone who doesn't believe in Father Christmas?

A rebel without a Claus.

Venezuela

The people of Caracas have an unusual way of getting to Midnight Mass on Christmas Eve: they roller skate. The streets of the capital are closed to traffic until the early hours of the morning so that the speed-loving worshippers can make their journey in safety. It is also traditional for the children of Caracas to tie a piece of string to one of their big toes before they go to bed and hang the other end out of the window, so that the roller skaters can wake them up by tugging on them as they pass. Just as effective as an alarm clock, but rather more painful, one would imagine.

Wales

Forget Santa. The Welsh have their own jolly festive figure in the shape of a horse's skull on a pole, carried by a person hidden from view under draped sheets. The Mari Lwyd wanders the streets accompanied by a band of singers and anyone who is 'bitten' by the skull has to pay a fine. It is also taken from house to house, where the merry group exchanges banter and insults with the householders.

Yugoslavia

In Yugoslavia, the second Sunday before Christmas is Mother's Day and is celebrated by children tying their mothers' legs to chairs while chanting, 'Mother's Day, Mother's Day, what will you pay to get away?' The little scamps are then given presents, which is all well and good, but not much fun for the poor mothers.

Pack Up Your Troubles

If the thought of yet another Christmas of last-minute panicking, endless chores and catering for ungrateful family members is getting you down, how about taking a trip of a lifetime and letting someone else do all the hard work? Here, for your consideration, are just a few of the top Christmas destinations around the world.

Lapland

Situated mostly in the Arctic Circle, the one thing you are guaranteed in Lapland is snow. Lots of it. At Christmas time it is very cold (temperatures can drop as low as $-40°C$) and constantly dark, but if you're lucky you might catch a glimpse of the magnificent Northern Lights.

As well as being the home of all things Santa-related, Lapland has plenty of other things to do, among them husky-dog safaris, cross-country skiing or hiking in one of the many national parks. The more adventurous should spend a night or two at the famous Icehotel in Swedish Lapland, where everything, including the beds, is made from ice. Brrr!

73

Rome

For a traditional Christmas steeped in culture, Rome is the place for you. Visit the impressive Christmas tree and life-sized Nativity scene in St Peter's Square, or the city's official crèche on the Spanish Steps. The atmospheric Midnight Mass in St Peter's Basilica is a must, as is the Pope's Christmas Day blessing. The famous Piazza Navona Christmas Market, with its stalls crammed with toys and edible goodies, is a treat for all the family. In true Italian style, food is all-important at this time of the year. Feast on the traditional Christmas Eve *capitone* – fried eel – and gorge on some of Italy's famous Christmas sweets made from honey and almonds.

New York

The Americans don't do things by halves, and Christmas is no exception. The holiday season kicks off in November with Macy's world-famous Thanksgiving Day Parade, an annual extravaganza that has taken place since 1924. The Rockefeller Center is the place to go for all things Christmassy. There you will find the Radio City Music Hall, which annually hosts a Christmas Spectacular from November to early January that is seen by more than a million people every year. The Rockefeller Center is also home to the mother of all Christmas trees, typically over sixty-five feet tall and decorated with over 25,000 lights, and its famous sunken ice-skating rink is one of the most popular Christmas destinations in the city.

Edinburgh

If non-stop partying is what you're after, take a break in Edinburgh. The Winter Festival begins in late November, with the switching on of the city's spectacular Christmas lights, and culminates in four days of Hogmanay revelry. The Winter Wonderland is the highlight of the festival, a heady mix of fairground rides, a huge outdoor skating rink and a traditional Christmas market. The annual Santa Run is great fun, too, with the city trying to break the record for the largest gathering of Santas running for charity.

Melbourne

If you're dreaming of a white Christmas then you'll probably want to give Christmas Down Under a miss. With temperatures that can soar to a sweltering 38°C(100°F), most Australians can be found on the beach roasting themselves rather than a turkey, hoping to catch a glimpse of Santa arriving on a surfboard or waterskis. If the idea of relaxing on the beach with a Christmas Day picnic lunch and a beer or two appeals to you, head to Melbourne. On Christmas Eve, tens of thousands of people gather under the stars for the spectacular Carols by Candlelight concert, held at the Sidney Myer Music Bowl.

Christmas Mondegreens

The term 'mondegreen' refers to commonly misheard sayings or lyrics and is attributed to writer Sylvia Wright, who had for years thought the lines 'They ha'e slain the Earl o' Murray, And they laid him on the green' from the Scottish ballad *The Bonny Earl o' Murray* were 'They ha'e slain the Earl Amurray, And Lady Mondegreen.'

I'm dreaming of a white Christmas,
Just like the wands I used to know.
Where the treetops glisten,
And children listen,
To hear **slave elves** in the snow.

Chipmunks roasting on an open fire,
Check for snipping at your nose.

Deck the halls with **Buddy Holly**
Fa la la la la la la la la.

The first Noel,
The angels did say,
Was to **frighten** poor shepherds
In fields where they lay.

25 December
1922

Lenin dictates his
Political Testament.

Get dressed, ye married gentlemen
Let nothing ye dismay.

Joy to the world!
The Lord **has gum.**

Silent night, holy night;
All is calm, all is bright.
Round John Virgin, margarine child
Holy imbecile, tender and mild.

While shepherd **washed their socks at** night,
All seated on the ground.

Hark **there Harold's angel** sings
Glory to the newborn **thing!**

CAROLLING

The word 'carol' comes from the Greek *choraulein*, a dance accompanied by flute music, and the French *caroller*, meaning 'to dance round in a circle'. Carols are said to have been introduced into church services in the twelfth century by St Francis of Assisi. At first they were sung at times of general celebration, but later they become associated specifically with the Nativity and were sung at Christmas.

The practice of carolling can be linked to ancient Rome and the Mummers, who were troupes of singers and dancers that went from house to house during the winter festival of Saturnalia. In the Middle Ages, wassailing, which comes from the old English term 'waes hael' meaning 'be well', was practised by peasants who visited their feudal lords at the beginning of each year to sing and bless their homes in exchange for wassail, a hot, spiced punch, and other favours. Although carolling today conjures up cosy images of wholesome children singing about the birth of Christ, some of the early songs have rather threatening overtones. Wassailers were often groups of rowdy young men who saw it as their right to gain favours from the wealthy at this time of year, and woe betide anyone who refused them entry:

> 'We have come to claim our right
> And if you don't open up your door,
> We'll lay you flat upon the floor.'

'Christmas gift suggestions:
To your enemy, forgiveness.
To an opponent, tolerance.
To a friend, your heart.
To a customer, service.
To all, charity.
To every child, a good example.
To yourself, respect.'

Oren Arnold

Tree Decorations

Although you can buy ornaments in every shape and colour under the sun, why not make a few of your own? It will add a personal touch to your tree and is a fun activity for the whole family. Here are just a couple of ideas to get the ball rolling.

Orange clove pomanders

Not only are these traditional pomanders attractive ornaments, but they also fill the house with a delicious, Christmassy fragrance. The spice mix adds even more scent, but you can leave it out if you prefer.

1. Wash some fresh oranges and pat them dry.

2. In a bowl, mix together equal amounts of ground cinnamon, ground nutmeg, allspice, ground cloves and orris root powder. The orris root acts as a preservative, making for a longer-lasting fragrance.

3. Stud the fruit with whole cloves, leaving about ¼ inch between each one. You can cover the whole orange evenly with cloves, or be a little more artistic and make a pattern.

4. Roll the studded oranges in the spice mix and leave them in a warm place to dry. It could take up to a month for them to dry out properly, so do this well in advance of Christmas.

5.   Once they are dry, tie ribbons around them or hook ornament hangers through the tops of the oranges and hang them on the tree.

Dough ornaments

Kids will love to help make these, and you can produce any shape you can think of, from angels to stars to reindeer. One batch of dough makes several ornaments. However, they're not edible, so don't be tempted to nibble them!

1.   In a bowl, mix together 16 oz (450 g) of plain flour and 8 oz (225 g) of salt. Slowly add cold water, mixing all the time, until you have a smooth dough. Roll out the dough on a floured surface until it is about ¼ inch thick.

2.   Draw the shapes you desire onto a piece of thick card and cut them out. Place the templates onto the dough and cut around them with a sharp knife. Make a hole at the top of each shape with a toothpick (ensuring the hole is big enough to thread string through) and place them on an ungreased baking tray. Bake in the oven, at the lowest setting, for a couple hours, or until the dough is hard but not brown.

25 December
1926

Hirohito becomes
Emperor of Japan.

3.   Once the shapes have cooled, use acrylic paints to decorate them as you wish. Thread some decorative string through the holes you made and hang them on the tree.

Wreath-making

For many people, wreaths are an integral part of Christmas-time decoration. Traditionally, they were a symbol of hope for the coming spring, with the evergreen foliage and the circular shape representing life during the dead of winter. You can hang your homemade wreaths on your door or walls, or use them as a decorative centrepiece for your table, with a candle placed in the middle.

It is possible to buy inexpensive wreath frames from florists, garden centres or craft shops, but it is easy to make your own by simply bending a wire coat hanger into a circular shape.

To create a traditional wreath, gather together various lengths of evergreen foliage and arrange them around the frame, using bits of thin wire to secure them.

Additional decorations can be attached with more wire or glue and can include all sorts of things: dried berries, pinecones and nuts (either in their natural state or spray-painted silver or gold), lengths of coloured ribbon, dried orange slices, cinnamon sticks, baubles, dried flowers and so on.

Hangover Cures

The endless Christmas festivities can take their toll, and pounding headaches and churning stomachs are just as much part of the holiday season as carols and snowmen. If you've woken up feeling like someone is repeatedly bashing you over the head with a hammer, give one of these tried and tested cures a go.

Hair of the dog

Your liver certainly won't thank you, but if you can stomach it, a bit of the hair of the dog that bit you is guaranteed to perk you up.

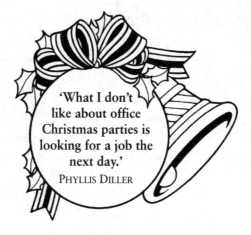

'What I don't like about office Christmas parties is looking for a job the next day.'
PHYLLIS DILLER

Bloody Mary (Serves 1)

The hangover classic. Probably so popular because the tomato juice and celery fools you into thinking you are being healthy.

2 measures vodka
200 ml tomato juice
Squeeze of lemon juice
2 dashes Worcestershire sauce

2 dashes Tabasco
Freshly ground pepper, to taste
1 celery stick

Place all the ingredients bar the celery stick into a cocktail shaker and shake well. Pour into a large glass filled with ice and garnish with the celery.

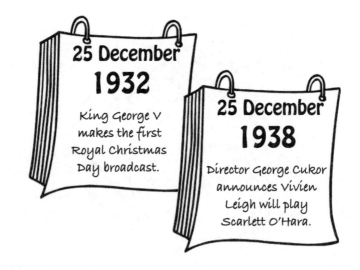

25 December 1932

King George V makes the first Royal Christmas Day broadcast.

25 December 1938

Director George Cukor announces Vivien Leigh will play Scarlett O'Hara.

Prairie Oyster (Serves 1)

This is not one for the faint-hearted, but some people swear by it. The prairie oyster is also said to be good for curing hiccups.

Dash of olive oil
1 egg yolk
1 measure port
Dash of Tabasco

2 dashes Worcestershire sauce
Squeeze of lemon juice
Salt and pepper, to taste

Drizzle the olive oil into a cocktail glass, swill it around and pour away the excess. Add the egg yolk, being careful not to break it as the idea is to swallow it whole. Add the rest of the ingredients, hold your nose and drink it down as fast as you can!

'Love came down at Christmas;
Love all lovely, love divine;
Love was born at Christmas,
Star and angels gave the sign.'

CHRISTINA ROSSETTI

Healthier options

Give your poor, suffering body a break and treat it like the temple it is.

❄ Alcohol leeches all sorts of nutrients and vitamins from your body, so the healthiest way to deal with the morning-after blues is to try to replace some of them. A big glass of ice-cold water with a vitamin tablet dissolved in it is a good idea, but if you can summon up the energy to prepare it, a vitamin-rich fruit smoothie will be even better and will also help to soothe your stomach. Just chop up the fruit and place in a blender with some yoghurt (to help settle your stomach), and some fruit juice (to thin the smoothie out a bit). Any fruit will do, but make sure you include some bananas. They are full of simple carbs, which will give you a quick energy boost and are high in potassium, which you lose a lot of when you drink. They are also a natural antacid, which will settle your stomach, and are rich in magnesium, which will help with your headache. The perfect hangover food.

❄ Many people swear by a good fry-up in the morning, but in truth what is essentially a plate of grease is unlikely to do your stomach any good, let alone your cholesterol levels. A much healthier option is simply some toast with Marmite, which is salty and therefore good for relieving nausea and will also provide some much-needed Vitamin B, or toast with honey, which is a good source of potassium and fructose.

❄ Water, water, water. Drink a lot, and when you think you can't swallow another drop, drink some more. Avoid coffee like the plague. The caffeine may give you an instant energy boost, but this won't last long and the stimulant will dehydrate you even more. Sports drinks will rehydrate you quickly and replace essential salts and minerals.

❄ It's really best to avoid painkillers altogether, as they just make your poor liver do even more work and will further irritate your already sensitive stomach. If you really must take something, stick to paracetamol rather than ibuprofen or aspirin. Never take painkillers before you go to bed, when there's still a lot of alcohol in your system.

Prevention is the best cure

Plan ahead and take it easy when you're out on the town and you'll be bounding out of bed the next morning, bright-eyed, bushy-tailed and ready to face the day ahead.

Before you go out:

❄ Line your stomach with something. A large glass of full-fat milk is a particularly good option as milk slows down the absorption of alcohol and fat is digested slowly and will help protect your stomach.

❄ Take a vitamin supplement that is high in Vitamins B and C.

While you are out:

❄ Alternate every alcoholic drink with something soft. Water and fruit juice are better than fizzy drinks, which actually help speed up the absorption of alcohol. For this reason, avoid fizzy drinks as mixers too.

❄ Some alcoholic drinks give you worse hangovers than others because they contain higher levels of impurities called congeners. A good rule of thumb is to avoid dark liquors such as rum, whisky and red wine and stick to white wine, vodka or gin.

Time for bed:

❄ Try to get some fresh air. If it's safe and convenient to walk home, do so. It will help to sober you up a bit.

❄ Eat something. Avoid the temptations of the local kebab shop and whip yourself up a simple bowl of carbohydrate-rich pasta. If fiddling about with boiling water and hot stoves is beyond you at this stage of the evening, a glass of milk and a banana will do just as well.

❄ Drink at least one large glass of water before you go to bed. It will be surprisingly difficult to get it down you, but your body will thank you for it in the morning.

Reindeer Facts

They may not be able to fly through the air and land gracefully and noiselessly on rooftops as festive legend would have it, but reindeer are surprising animals, nonetheless.

❄ Both male and female reindeer have antlers, the only species of deer to display this trait, and every reindeer grows a new set annually.

❄ Unless they are castrated, male reindeer shed their antlers at the beginning of winter and females shed theirs in spring. Therefore, all Santa's reindeer must be either female or castrated males. Assuming the latter, poor Rudolph. I'm not sure having a shiny nose makes up for that.

❄ The people of the Lapp tribe in northern Scandinavia believe that powdered reindeer antlers increase virility.

❄ Rudolph of red-nosed fame was originally going to be named either Rollo or Reginald, until creator Robert May's four-year-old daughter Barbara expressed a preference for Rudolph.

❄ Reindeer have been around for a long time. Ice Age engravings in a cave in France depict what is thought to be reindeer, and the artwork has been dated from 12,000 to 10,500 BC.

❄ Reindeer don't sink into the snow despite their size because their weight is distributed over a large area due to their wide, splayed hooves.

❄ Reindeer are mostly herbivores, feeding on grasses, mosses, leaves and lichens, but they also supplement their diets with rodents, eggs, placenta and shed antlers when greenery is in short supply.

❄ A reindeer can pull twice its body weight for up to forty miles.

25 December
1939

Department store Montgomery Ward introduces Rudolph the Red-nosed Reindeer to the world.

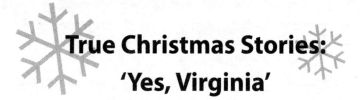

True Christmas Stories: 'Yes, Virginia'

In 1897, eight-year-old Virginia O'Hanlon wrote the following letter to Francis P. Church, the Editor of the *New York Sun*.

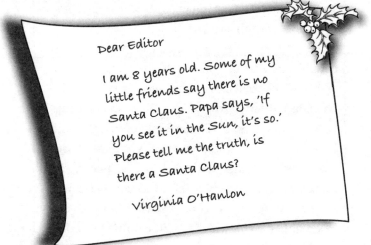

Dear Editor

I am 8 years old. Some of my little friends say there is no Santa Claus. Papa says, 'If you see it in the Sun, it's so.' Please tell me the truth, is there a Santa Claus?

Virginia O'Hanlon

The Editor's reply became instantly famous and more than one hundred years later it continues to be the most reprinted editorial ever to run in an English-language newspaper.

Virginia, your little friends are wrong. They have been affected by the scepticism of a sceptical age. They do not believe except they see. They think that nothing can be which is not comprehensible by their little minds. All minds, Virginia, whether they be men's or children's, are little. In this great universe of ours, man is a mere insect, an ant, in his intellect as compared with the boundless world about him, as measured by the intelligence capable of grasping the whole of truth and knowledge.

Yes, Virginia, there is a Santa Claus. He exists as certainly as love and generosity and devotion exist, and you know that they abound and give to your life its highest beauty and joy. Alas! How dreary would be the world if there were no Santa Claus! It would be as dreary as if there were no Virginias. There would be no childlike faith then, no poetry, no romance to make tolerable this existence. We should have no enjoyment, except in sense and sight. The external light with which childhood fills the world would be extinguished.

Not believe in Santa Claus! You might as well not believe in fairies. You might get your papa to hire men to watch in all the chimneys on Christmas Eve to catch Santa Claus, but even if you did not see Santa Claus coming down, what would that prove? Nobody sees Santa Claus, but that is no sign that there is no Santa Claus. The most real things in the world are those that neither children nor men can see. Did you ever see fairies dancing on the lawn? Of course not, but that's no proof that they are not there. Nobody can conceive or imagine all the wonders there are unseen and unseeable in the world. You tear apart the baby's rattle and see what makes the noise inside, but there is a veil covering the unseen world which not the strongest man, nor even the united strength of all the strongest men that ever lived could tear apart. Only faith, poetry, love, romance, can push aside that curtain and view and picture the supernal beauty and glory beyond.

Is it all real? Ah, Virginia, in all this world there is nothing else real and abiding.

No Santa Claus? Thank God he lives and lives forever. A thousand years from now, Virginia, nay 10 times 10,000 years from now, he will continue to make glad the heart of childhood.

Merry Christmas and a Happy New Year!!!!

25 December
1941

Hong Kong surrenders to the Japanese.

25 December
1950

The Stone of Scone is stolen from Westminster Abbey by four Scottish students.

Christmas Practical Jokes

Goodwill to all men is all well and good, but having a laugh at someone else's expense is always fun, and Christmas is all about enjoying yourself, after all. Just pick your victims well and don't expect much in the way of presents from them this year.

❄ Sick of that co-worker who always jets off on an expensive Caribbean holiday just before Christmas to top-up their tan for the party season? While they're away, painstakingly gift-wrap everything on, and in, their desk: computer monitor, mouse, individual pens, stapler, phone . . . you get the picture. And use lurid wrapping paper, with lots of sticky tape.

❄ Make the biggest snowball you possibly can – we're talking *huge* here. Get a friend or two to help out. When it's done, haul it up to your victim's bedroom and place it in the middle of their bed. Turn off the heating and open the window so that it doesn't melt too fast. Refuse to help as your victim frantically tries to get rid of it before their bed sheets get totally soaked.

❄ If you've received one of those annoying Christmas cards that play a jingle every time you open it, take it apart and remove the music chip. Attach it to the hinge of a door (a wardrobe door works well) so that it activates whenever the door is opened. Your victim won't be able to work out where it is coming from, and those chips keep going for a long time . . .

❄ This is great fun if you're feeling a little mischievous during a family Christmas party. Choose your 'victim', sit them on a chair, and explain to them that you'd like them to take part in a blindfolded co-ordination test; a test, incidentally, that only the very brightest succeed at. Sit in front of the victim and hold up your hands, palms facing, about a ruler's width apart. Now, ask your friend or relative to place their hands together and pass them between your hands and back out again, without touching your hands in the process. This counts as '1', you inform them, and the smartest people can do this forty or fifty times. Now they've practised, remind them that the test must be conducted blindfolded. Once this is done, resume the position of your hands, ask them to start, and remind them to count upwards as they do so. After thirty seconds or so, walk quietly away and watch them rock their hands back and forth, counting to themselves, like someone possessed . . . Just try not to laugh! Encourage others to come and have a look!

❄ When the temperature plummets, sneak out late one night and fill your victim's outdoor rubbish bins with water, which will quickly become a couple of hundred pounds of solid ice.

❄ When it's time for the annual nightmare that is the office 'Secret Santa', replace all the slips of paper with your co-workers' names on them with slips on which only your own name appears. Reap the rewards, and then look for a new job.

❄ Take two sticky notes and write 'Merry Christmas!' on them. Place one or two of these notes on the glass of the office photocopier, put the lid down and press the 'Copy' button. Move the notes and repeat, and do this several times, and finally throw the notes away. When the sheets of paper emerge with the festive message printed on them, take these sheets and put them back into the paper trays. Now, watch as the unsuspecting victim uses the photocopier, picks up their copies . . . and sees the mysterious notes on their documents. Have a chuckle to yourself when they open the lid and search in vain for the source of these spooky Yuletide messages that are mysteriously appearing!

❄ Dress up like the Easter Bunny and pick a fight with a department-store Santa, telling him that 'this town ain't big enough for the both of us.'

❄ Liven up a dull Christmas party by addressing all the men as 'Mrs' and the women as 'Mr'.

'From a commercial point of view, if Christmas did not exist it would be necessary to invent it.'
KATHARINE WHITEHORN

Hosting a Christmas Party (2)

Our guide to throwing the best knees-up in town continues.

Being a good host

Being a good host means making sure that things run smoothly and that your guests are adequately fed and watered and are mingling happily, rather than standing around awkwardly staring at the floor. It doesn't mean rushing around like a headless chicken, fretting about every little thing and panicking when something goes wrong. If you are uptight, your guests will be too. If you feel yourself getting anxious, take a deep breath, have a couple of drinks and relax. It's your party; you should enjoy it too! If you're hosting the party on your own, rope in a couple of friends to help out with handing out nibbles and keeping glasses topped up.

Make an effort to greet each and every guest as they arrive. This doesn't mean you have to hover by the front door all night waiting for stragglers. Just be alert and listen out for the doorbell. Immediately offer them a drink, listing what is available. If you just say, 'What would you like to drink?' most people will reply, 'Oh, whatever you've got open,' and might then be stuck with a drink they don't like.

If your guests don't all know each other, make the necessary introductions. Always be on the lookout for people who are standing alone. If you spot someone on their own, perhaps lead them over to a group and introduce a topic of conversation to which you know they will be able to contribute.

Be responsible about how much your guests are drinking. If you see that someone is drinking very quickly, fill up their glass only halfway next time, or offer them a soft drink. If a guest looks a little the worse for wear and is planning on driving home, don't turn a blind eye. Insist on calling them a cab or ask around to see if someone can give them a lift home. If necessary, and assuming you have the space, consider offering them a bed or sofa for the night. They'll thank you in the morning!

Alcohol

It's always tricky to calculate how much booze to order in for a party. As a rough guide, allow for about five drinks per person for a reasonably lengthy party. A 75 cl bottle of wine provides six drinks and a 75 cl bottle of spirits should be enough for about forty. Bear in mind that many people will bring a bottle or two along (it's absolutely fine to ask people on your invitation to bring alcohol with them, by the way). Don't go overboard on the spirits. There should be a few staples available, but you don't want to be mixing a variety of fancy cocktails all night. Make sure there is an abundance of soft drinks available.

Consider providing:

Red and white wine
Beer
Vodka
Whisky
Rum
Gin
Orange juice
Cranberry juice
Coke
Soda and tonic water
Mineral water

25 December
1957

The Royal Christmas Day message is broadcast on television for the first time.

Make sure you have plenty of ice. Buy a few party bags of pre-made ice from the supermarket and make some room for them in your freezer. Place an ice-bucket near the booze and keep it topped up throughout the night.

Consider ordering your alcohol from one of the big off-licence chains. Many have a 'sale or return' policy, which means any unopened bottles will not have to be paid for. If you do this, make sure you put out bottles only as you need them, to avoid being stuck with ten half-full bottles at the end of the evening. Also, don't forget to provide enough glasses. If you do order your drink from an off-licence they may hire out glassware, often for free, depending on the size of your order.

Food

You'll need to provide plenty of food to soak up all that alcohol. Finger food is by far the best option as your guests won't have to queue while performing complicated balancing acts with plates, knives and forks and glasses. Just make sure you provide plenty of napkins and keep the food circulating throughout the evening.

You should allow about ten canapés or nibbles per person – you'll probably have leftovers, but it's better to have too much food than not enough. Buy some cheap disposable containers so that you can offer leftovers to guests as they leave if you have a lot of surplus food. Serve a good variety of nibbles and plenty of vegetarian options.

All supermarkets stock pre-made party bites, so there's absolutely no need to cook everything yourself, but if you do want to impress your guests with your culinary skills, choose food that can be prepared in advance and served cold or heated up at the last minute. Below are a few suggestions for nibbles that are a little bit different . . .

Cranberry filo rolls (Makes 15 to 20 rolls)

50 g (2 oz) dried cranberries
50 g (2 oz) ground almonds
1 tbsp capers in vinegar, drained
1 tbsp fresh dill, chopped

½ tsp cumin seeds
3 small sheets filo pastry
25 g (1 oz) butter, melted

1. Preheat the oven to 220°C/425°F/Gas mark 7.

2. Put the dried cranberries in a bowl, cover them with boiling water and leave them to soak for about 20 minutes. When they are soft, drain them and put them in a food processor along with the ground almonds, capers, dill and cumin seeds. Blend until you have a purée.

3. Lay out a sheet of filo pastry and brush it with the melted butter. Spoon a strip of the cranberry mixture along the bottom of the pastry, about an inch above the edge. Fold the bottom edge over the filling and then continue to roll until you have a tight tube. Cut off the two ends and then cut into 2-inch-wide pieces. Repeat this with the other sheets of pastry, then place them on a baking tray and bake for 15 to 20 minutes, until golden. Can be served straight from the oven or cold.

Bruschetta with peppers and pesto
(Makes 15 to 20 pieces)

For the bruschetta
2 baguettes
3 garlic cloves, peeled
Olive oil, for drizzling

For the peppers
6 red peppers
6 garlic cloves, finely chopped
5 shallots, finely chopped
Juice of 2 lemons
1 tsp dried oregano
5 tbsp olive oil
3 tbsp sherry vinegar
Salt
Freshly ground black pepper
1 jar pesto

1. Pre-heat the oven to 200°C/400°F/Gas mark 6.

2. Cut the bread into slices that are about half an inch thick. Rub one side of each slice all over with the whole garlic cloves and drizzle with olive oil. Place on a baking tray and bake for 2 to 3 minutes, until they are golden brown. Remove from the oven and leave to cool.

3. Put the whole peppers on a baking tray and bake them for about 30 minutes, or until they are blackened. Remove them from the oven and immediately put them into a plastic bag, seal it and leave them to cool. Once cool, it should be easy to peel off the skins. Cut them into long strips, discarding the core and seeds.

4. In a bowl, mix together the garlic, shallots, lemon juice, oregano, olive oil and sherry vinegar. Season to taste, add the peppers, toss everything together and set aside for a couple of hours.

5. When you are ready to serve, simply top each bruschetta with some peppers and a dollop of pesto.

Prosciutto parcels (Makes 25 parcels)

400 g (14 oz) sliced prosciutto ham
200 g (7 oz) dried figs
150 g (5½ oz) mild, soft goat's cheese

Cut each slice of prosciutto into three strips. Slice each fig in half, spread with a small dollop of goat's cheese and fold them in the strips of prosciutto to form parcels.

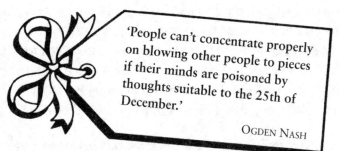

'People can't concentrate properly on blowing other people to pieces if their minds are poisoned by thoughts suitable to the 25th of December.'

OGDEN NASH

THE YULE LOG

The origins of the Yule log can be traced back to the Norsemen of northern Europe. *Jol* or *Jule* (pronounced 'Yule') was a festival celebrated on the Winter Solstice in honour of Jolnir, also known as Odin, the god of intoxicating drink, ecstasy and death. Feasting and drinking would take place around bonfires and fires would be lit in hearths.

This tradition spread to other parts of Europe, where tree-worship was already part of pagan rituals. Households would venture into the woods on Christmas Eve and cut a log from an oak tree, which was then transported home, with much singing and merrymaking along the way. The log would be put on the fire, which would be kept burning for twelve days, and it was believed to bring health and productivity to the family and their crops for the coming year and protect them from witchcraft and demons. When the fire was finally extinguished a small piece of the wood would be kept and used to light the next year's log. Often the ashes would be scattered over the fields in order to ensure fertility.

Later on, the Yule log was used as a decorative centrepiece for the Christmas table, and as stoves replaced the giant household hearths, the pastry or chocolate logs we are familiar with today came into being.

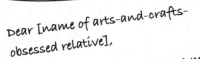

Dear [name of arts-and-crafts-obsessed relative],

Every year I await your home-made gift with a sense of breathless anticipation. This Christmas, as always, I was not disappointed. The jumper is superb. Who would have thought that neon pink, brown and orange would make for such a successful colour combination? How clever of you to knit it several sizes too big! You just never know when you might be hit by one of those mid-life growth spurts. I shall wear it with pride in the privacy of my own home.

Yours sincerely,

Fun and Games

Whether you want to break the ice at a party or simply keep the kids entertained and away from the television, it's always good to have a few fun games and group activities up your sleeve at Christmas.

For the kids

❄ Ask each child to gather together a selection of small household items and wrap them in leftover scraps of wrapping paper. They then swap their items and get a point for each item they correctly guess without unwrapping them.

❄ Write down a list of anagrams of Christmas words on a sheet of paper and get the children to unscramble as many as they can within a certain time limit, with a prize going to the one who gets the most right.

❄ Pin a white sheet of paper to the wall and place a chair facing it. Position a table behind the chair with a lit lamp on it, shining towards the wall. Each child takes turns to sit in the chair, while the others walk between the lamp and chair one by one. The child who is seated must guess who walked across by their shadow.

❄ Place a chair in the middle of the room with a set of keys underneath it. One child is blindfolded and sits in the chair. The others must take turns to sneak up to the chair, steal the keys and return to the starting line without making any noise. If the blindfolded child hears anything, the person attempting the theft is out of the game. The child who gets the furthest is the winner and takes their turn in the chair.

❄ Get two children to mime a scene – driving a car, playing tennis, or rowing a boat, for example. At some point shout 'Stop!', at which the actors must freeze in the position they were in. Another child then takes the place of one of the actors and must adopt the exact same position. They must then improvise a different scene according to the positions they are in.

❄ Put an assortment of adult-sized clothes into separate bags. Give one bag to each child. On the word 'Go!' they must put on every item in the bag over their own clothes. The winner is the one who dresses the fastest.

❄ Tear out pages from a magazine that display a complete image on them. Cut each page into smaller pieces to form a jigsaw. Place each 'jigsaw' in a bag or box and hand one to each team. The winning team is the one that completes their jigsaw first.

❄ Blow up one balloon per child and write their name on it. Hand out a balloon, and a flat sheet of paper to each child. The object of the game is to keep the balloon in the air for as long as possible, using only the paper to waft it.

❄ Organize an indoor treasure hunt. Prepare a 'goodie bag' containing sweets or small stocking-filler gifts for

107

each child. Hide each bag in a separate location, along with a clue to lead them to the next goodie bag. Start them off on their group hunt by handing them a written clue to where they can find the first bag.

❄ Each participant chooses the name of a local railway station and makes this known to the other players. Everyone sits down in a circle except one person who stands in the middle. The person in the middle then says, for example, 'This Christmas I went from Paddington to Liverpool Street.' The two people who are called Paddington and Liverpool Street then must exchange places as fast as possible, while the person in the middle attempts to take over one of the empty places. Every so often the person in the middle can shout 'all change', upon which everyone must get up and swap places, and the player left without a seat must stay in the middle.

❄ Divide everyone up into two teams. Attach two spoons to very long pieces of string and give one to each team. The two teams then line up facing each other and on the word 'go' they must link themselves together by passing their spoon along the line. The spoon must be passed down the clothes of one team member and then up the clothes of the next team member. The quickest team wins.

❄ Each player (or victim!) takes turns to be blindfolded. Another player holds their nose while feeding them either a slice of cooked sprout or a piece of chocolate truffle. The victim has to guess what they are actually eating. Guessing is harder than it seems, because it's difficult to taste anything when your nose is being held!

For the adults

❄ Ask everyone to sit in a circle and take turns to stand in the middle and make three statements about themselves, one of which must be a lie. Everyone must then guess which statement is the lie.

❄ Provide each guest with five small pieces of paper and a pencil and ask them to write down the names of five famous people. Fold the pieces of paper and place them in a hat or box. Divide everyone into groups of two and ask one person to pick a piece of paper. That person must provide clues as to the celebrity's identity until their partner gets it right, without mentioning the person's name. Each couple has thirty seconds to guess as many as they can and a point is awarded for every correct answer.

❄ Another variation of the 'name game' involves asking everyone to write down the name of a famous person on a piece of paper. Jumble the names up and hand one out to each guest. Get people mingling and chatting, but they must act in character while others try to guess who they are supposed to be.

25 December
1973

Scot Tommy Chambers completes his 51-year cycle tour of 799,405 miles.

Which Christmas carol do new parents like best?

'Silent Night'.

❄ Choose four people to start off this game. Three of the four leave the room and the fourth is asked by the host to mime out a scene. It should be something unusual and difficult to act, such as trying to break into a locked car or stepping into a bath full of custard. One of the group is then called back in and watches the mime. The original 'actor' then sits back down and the second of the group then has to mime what he thinks he just saw to the next person in the group, and so it continues. After watching the third mime attempt, the final person in the group then has to say what he thinks the scene is all about.

❄ Each player is given a piece of paper with columns headed with categories such as: girl's name, boy's name, country, city, river, tree, animal, book, film, etc. One person then randomly chooses a letter of the alphabet and every participant must write down one thing that begins with that letter for each section. The game stops when one person has finished – it's a race against everyone else. Players are awarded one point if someone else has also got the same answer and two points for a unique answer.

'Christmas at my house is always at least six or seven times more pleasant than anywhere else. We start drinking early. And while everyone else is seeing only one Santa Claus, we'll be seeing six or seven.'

W. C. FIELDS

❄ A game for two teams, with each team given a piece of paper on which is an example of the following appears: a contagious disease, a garden tool, a female celebrity, an unusual holiday destination, a small, furry animal, a part of the anatomy, something you'd use to clean the kitchen, a UK tabloid newspaper, a cartoon character, a traditional Christmas foodstuff, a UK music group, and the name of one of Santa's reindeers. With this information, each team must then spend ten minutes writing an alternative Queen's Christmas Speech in the fashion of Her Majesty, which mentions each item on the list in order – and they must then perform the speech. Award marks for creativity, delivery and sheer enthusiasm.

❄ All players must sit in a circle. The first participant chooses an adverb – such as humorously, happily, excitedly, mournfully, and so on – and whispers it to the player sitting to their right. This player then has to sing a Christmas carol in the manner of the chosen word until the other players have guessed the adverb. Pick some amusing adverbs and watch the theatrical side of your friends and family members shine through!

What did the bald man say when he got a comb for Christmas?

'Thanks, I'll never part with it.'

Present-wrapping Made Easy (2)

In part two of our guide to gift-wrapping we look at those decorative touches that can make all the difference.

Beautiful bows

Bows are a particularly attractive addition to any package. Most of the gift-wrapping ribbon (i.e. non-fabric ribbon) on sale is curling ribbon, and can be used to make these pretty decorations. To curl a strand of ribbon, open up a pair of scissors and run the blunt edge along the entire length of the ribbon. This looks very attractive when applied to the ribbon used to secure the tube and wine bottle in the methods detailed on pages 26 and 27. In addition, follow the steps below to add a curling ribbon bow to a wrapped box.

1. Cut several long strands of thin ribbon; the more ribbon you use, the more extravagant your bow. Using different colours and textures can work well. Hold them together and use them as if they were one strand.

2. Make sure the box is laid in front of you the right way up and place the ribbon over the top.

3. Turn the box around, so that the ribbon is now under the box, and bring the two ends up to the middle. Twist them around each other, then go around the box in the other direction, flipping it over so that it is the right way round again.

4. Secure the ends together by tying a tight double knot, then tie the ribbon into a large bow.

5. Cut through the middle of each of the bow's loops and curl each strand as detailed above.

Alternatively, you can use a thicker ribbon to produce a more unusual bow that goes around each corner of the box, rather than the middle.

1. Cut a long length of flat, wide ribbon.

2. Place your wrapped box the right way round in front of you and place the ribbon so that it is diagonally over the top left corner of the box, making sure you leave a long tail.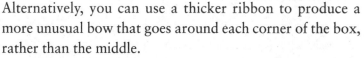

3. Hold the ribbon in place and take it round the back of the box and then back over the front of the bottom right corner.

4. Take the ribbon round the back of the bottom left corner and then back over the front to where you started.

5. Secure the ends together by tying a tight double knot, then tie into a bow.

'Christmas is forced upon a reluctant and disgusted nation by the shopkeepers and the press; on its own merits it would wither and shrivel in the fiery breath of universal hatred.'

GEORGE BERNARD SHAW

Fabric gift bags

If you've followed these tips and are still finding yourself covered head to toe in pieces of sticky tape and surrounded by a sea of torn and crumpled wrapping paper, try whizzing up a few quick and easy fabric gift bags. All you need are some scraps of colourful material and some plain cotton for the lining (old bed sheets work well).

Cut two pieces of fabric and two pieces of the lining material to size (1). Put one piece of fabric over each piece of lining, fold over the top edges and sew a hem. This will form the top of the gift bag (2).

Put the pieces of material together so that the lining is facing the outside, and sew the three unhemmed sides together (3).

Turn the bag inside out. Attach a ribbon a couple of inches down from the top of the bag by sewing a few stitches in the middle of the ribbon, at the back of the bag (4).

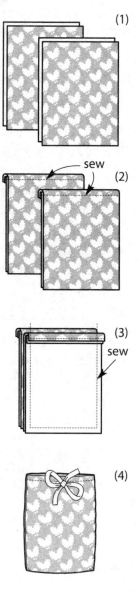

Creative ideas

If you're feeling adventurous, get creative and try something a little bit different. Here are just a few suggestions:

❄ Join together leftover scraps of wrapping paper in contrasting colours and textures and re-use. You can disguise any messy joins with ribbons.

❄ Experiment with other types of paper. Newspaper, for example, may seem like a cheap option, but it looks fantastic when teamed up with a luxurious fabric-ribbon bow in a bright colour. Pages from the Sunday papers' comic supplements are perfect for wrapping children's presents. Plain brown paper works well when tied up with a length of white gauze or a natural material such as raffia.

❄ Make your own personalized wrapping paper by typing out an appropriate dictionary definition on a piece of blank paper (e.g. 'Santa Claus, *n*., the legendary patron saint of children') and using a photocopier to enlarge it, or assembling and printing out a collage of family photographs.

❄ Match gifts with appropriate containers. For example, gardening gloves can be presented in a terracotta pot, or kitchen implements in a colourful oven glove.

❄ Make attractive gift boxes for small items out of egg cartons. Cut two sections out and tape them together on one side to form a hinge. Decorate them with paint, glitter, stickers or anything else you can think of. Fill with tissue paper and pop the gift in.

❄ There are a multitude of things you can use to embellish your package. Dried or silk flowers, bits of holly or mistletoe, miniature pine cones and dried leaves are great for a natural look. Add a feminine touch by wrapping a bead necklace around the gift instead of ribbon. Striped candy canes are colourful adornments that can be enjoyed in other ways once Christmas lunch has been digested. The only limit is your imagination!

What do they call Santa's helpers?

Subordinate Clauses.

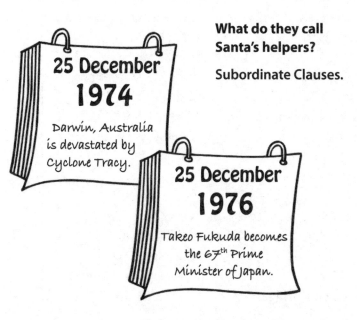

25 December 1974

Darwin, Australia is devastated by Cyclone Tracy.

25 December 1976

Takeo Fukuda becomes the 67th Prime Minister of Japan.

Christmas Place Names

If the idea of an all-year-round Christmas appeals, consider moving to one of the many festively named spots around the world, where the celebration will never be far from your mind.

Bethlehem	Carmarthenshire, Wales
Blitzen	Oregon, USA
Christmas Creek	Australia
Christmas Cross	Shropshire, England
Christmas Gift Mine	Arizona, USA
Christmas Island	Australia
Cold Christmas	Hertfordshire, England
Cranberry	Staffordshire, England
Eggnog	Utah, USA
Elf	North Carolina, USA
Holly Green	Worcestershire, England
Jolly	Texas, USA
Merry Christmas Creek	Alaska, USA
Mistletoe Oak	Herefordshire, England
Noel	Louisiana, USA
North Pole	Alaska, USA
Plum Pudding Creek	New Zealand
Rudolph	Wisconsin, USA
Santa Claus	Indiana, USA
Star	Somerset, England
Stocking	Herefordshire, England
Wiseman's Bridge	Pembrokeshire, Wales

Gift Ideas

It can be a struggle to think of original and appropriate gifts each year. Give plenty of thought to the person you are buying for. What are their hobbies? Do they have any passions? If in doubt, confer with someone who knows them better than you do. Try to think outside the box and avoid anonymous gifts like toiletries and scented candles. If you're still stuck, check out the tips below for some inspiration.

Children

❄ Avoid anything to do with the latest crazes. They'll be over before the toy is even out of the box.

❄ Always check the manufacturer's age guidelines before buying a toy.

❄ Avoid very noisy or disruptive toys if you want to remain friendly with the child's parents.

❄ Never buy a child a pet without first consulting the parents.

CONSIDER

❄ Ice-skating or horse-riding lessons.

❄ Membership to a local zoo. Many zoos offer animal adoption programmes. Kids will love visiting their adopted animal and receiving photos and updates.

❄ Classic board games such as Monopoly or Snakes and Ladders.

❄ A nicely bound set of classic children's books.

❄ A chemistry set or magic kit.

❄ A piggy bank with some money in it to start them off.

❄ Personalized stationery.

❄ A subscription to a favourite comic.

Teenagers

❄ Avoid any fashion-related gifts unless it's something they specifically pointed out and asked for. Chances are you'll get it wrong!

❄ Check with the parents as to what is and isn't allowed in the household before you buy anything that could be controversial.

CONSIDER

❄ Gift certificates from a favourite clothes or music store.

❄ Vouchers to download music.

❄ Pay-as-you-go mobile-phone top-ups.

❄ A diary or scrapbook.

❄ Sports equipment.

❄ College fund or savings-account contributions.

❄ Tickets to a gig.

❄ Cinema vouchers.

Friends and Family

❄ Avoid domestic appliances like the plague! As a general rule, if it's got a plug, don't buy it.

❄ As with teenagers, it's best to avoid clothes or jewellery unless you are very sure of the person's tastes.

CONSIDER

❄ Activity-related gifts. Activity-day websites offer an enormous variety of pre-paid activities, from racing-car driving to spa days to cookery courses.

❄ A donation to a favourite charity.

❄ Theatre vouchers.

❄ Newspaper or magazine subscriptions.

❄ Museum memberships.

❄ Travel vouchers.

❄ A newspaper from the day the person was born.

❄ A photo album you've put together of favourite family snaps.

❄ Tickets to sporting events.

❄ Memorabilia such as sports programmes, autographs and film posters. Check Internet auction sites for these.

Colleagues and Neighbours

❄ Don't overdo it on gifts for people you don't know very well. It will make them feel awkward, particularly if they haven't got you anything.

CONSIDER

❄ Home-made edible gifts. Try something a little bit different, rather than the usual batch of mince pies. See pages 124–7 for inspiration.

❄ Christmas tree ornaments.

❄ A bulb planted in an attractive container that will flower in time for Christmas.

❄ A bottle of wine or spirits.

'Mankind is a great, an immense family . . . This is proved by what we feel in our hearts at Christmas.'
POPE JOHN XXIII

Edible Gifts

Everybody likes to indulge at Christmas time. These naughty but nice nibbles will go down a treat.

Chocolate truffles

200 g (7 oz) good dark chocolate
200 ml (7 fl. oz) double cream
Cocoa powder for dusting

1. Break the chocolate into chunks and place in a bowl over a pan of simmering water. Slowly melt the chocolate down, stirring all the time.

2. Gently heat the cream in a saucepan until it is warm. Pour the cream over the chocolate, stir in well and leave to cool and set.

3. Once set, take teaspoons of the mixture, dust with cocoa powder and roll into balls.

How does Good King Wenceslas like his pizzas?

Deep pan, crisp and even.

Fudge

300 ml (10½ fl. oz) full-fat milk   1 tsp vanilla extract
350 g (12 oz) caster sugar   Oil, for greasing
100 g (3½ oz) unsalted butter

1. Heat the milk, sugar and butter together in a saucepan over a very low heat, stirring all the time, until the sugar has dissolved.

2. Bring to the boil and stir constantly. After 15 minutes, test that the fudge is ready by dropping a small amount into a bowl of cold water – it should form a soft ball.

3. Remove the mixture from the heat and add the vanilla extract. Let it cool down a bit, then beat it with a wooden spoon until it starts to thicken.

4. Pour it into a greased, square cake tin and allow it to set at room temperature before cutting it into squares.

Shortbread

225 g (8 oz) caster sugar
450 g (16 oz) butter
Pinch of salt

450 g (16 oz) plain flour
225 g (8 oz) rice flour
Granulated sugar, for sprinkling

1. Beat the sugar into the butter until the mixture is creamy and fluffy. In a separate bowl, mix together the salt, plain flour and rice flour, then thoroughly combine with the butter mixture.

2. Form the mixture into a ball, then roll it by hand into a tube that is about 2 to 3 inches in diameter. Wrap the tube in cling film and leave in the fridge until it is hard.

3. Preheat the oven to 190°C/375°F/Gas mark 5. Unwrap the tube and cut into half-inch-thick slices. Sprinkle with granulated sugar and bake for about 20 minutes, until the shortbread is very slightly golden. Cool on a wire rack.

25 December
1977

Israel's Prime Minister Menachem Begin and Egyptian President Anwar al-Sadat begin peace talks at Ismailia in Egypt.

Limoncello

This delicious home-made version of the Italian liqueur takes about a month to develop its full flavour, so make it well ahead of Christmas.

200 g (7 oz) caster sugar
150 ml (5 fl. oz) water

6 lemons, juice and zest
700 ml (24½ fl. oz) vodka

1. Dissolve the sugar into the water over a low heat, then bring to the boil and simmer for about 3 to 4 minutes until it forms a syrup.

2. Allow it to cool a little and, while it is still warm, add the lemon juice and zest and the vodka. Mix well and pour into sterilized bottles.

3. Keep them in a cool, dark place and give them a shake every day for the first week, to make sure all the ingredients are well blended.

4. Leave untouched for about four weeks, by which time its flavour will be just right.
Serve very cold, straight from the fridge, and enjoy!

HOLLY AND IVY

Like mistletoe, holly and ivy were important to the ancient Europeans. The fact that they are evergreen plants meant that they were thought of as magical, representing eternal life and the cycle of nature and giving hope for the coming spring. They were used together in rites because they were said to represent the masculine (holly) and feminine (ivy) elements of nature. This then led to both holly and ivy being introduced into the home to create harmony and balance.

Holly is also associated with the Roman winter festival of Saturnalia, in honour of the god Saturn, which was celebrated much as we celebrate Christmas today, with fervent merrymaking and homes being decorated with evergreen plants.

The early Christians associated holly with Christ, with the sharp-edged leaves representing his crown of thorns and the red berries his shed blood.

Leftover Turkey

It happens every year. You buy the biggest turkey you can find for Christmas lunch and are then faced with days of endless turkey sandwiches. Try some of the quick and easy recipes below if you fancy using up all that meat and making something a little bit different.

Potted turkey (Serves 4 to 6)

This is an easy pâté to make and is delicious served with salad and wholemeal toast. It also freezes very well.

> 80 g (3 oz) butter
> 225 g (8 oz) white and dark cooked turkey meat, roughly chopped
> ¼ tsp cayenne pepper
> Nutmeg, freshly grated
>
> ¼ lemon, juiced
> Salt and freshly ground black pepper
> 30 g (1 oz) unsalted butter

1. Melt the butter in a saucepan, taking care not to let it brown. Add the turkey meat, cayenne pepper, nutmeg and lemon juice, and heat through. Place the mixture in a food processor and blend until the consistency is medium-coarse. Season to taste.

2. Pack the mixture tightly into ramekins, making sure you leave room at the top for the clarified butter (see point 3) and put in the fridge to chill for at least a couple of hours.

3. After the pâté has cooled down and set in the fridge, melt the unsalted butter over a gentle heat and allow it to cool. Skim off any foam that rises to the surface and pour the clarified butter over the ramekins to seal the pâté. Return the ramekins to the fridge and leave there until the butter has set.

'There is a remarkable breakdown of taste and intelligence at Christmas time. Mature, responsible grown men wear neckties made of holly leaves and drink alcoholic beverages with raw egg yolks and cottage cheese in them.'

P. J. O'ROURKE

Why was Santa's little helper depressed?

He had low elf-esteem.

Turkey empanadas (Serves 4)

A delicious alternative to turkey sandwiches. If you like a bit of heat, use the small, fiery red chillies; for a sweeter, milder flavour go with the larger green ones.

225 g (8 oz) white and dark cooked turkey meat, roughly chopped	55 g (2 oz) cornmeal
	½ tsp salt
250 g (9 oz) cheddar cheese, grated	80 g (3 oz) butter
110 g (4 oz) chillies, chopped	55 ml (2 fl. oz) cold water
225 g (8 oz) wholewheat flour	1 tbsp milk

1. Preheat the oven to 200°C/400°F/Gas mark 6.

2. Mix together the turkey, cheese and chillies in a bowl and set aside.

3. In another bowl combine the flour, cornmeal and salt. Mix in the butter, a bit at a time, until the mixture is crumbly, then slowly add the water, mixing all the time, until you have a dough.

4. Divide the dough into two balls and roll out one on a floured surface. Place half of the turkey mixture over half of the pastry, leaving about 2 inches of pastry along the edges. Fold the other half of the pastry over the turkey mixture, crimp the edges together to seal them and brush with the milk. Repeat this process with the other ball of dough.

5. Place the empanadas on a greased baking tray and bake for about 25 minutes, or until they are golden brown.

Turkey chow mein (Serves 4)

Despite the long list of ingredients, this is a quick, easy and healthy dish to prepare.

120 ml (4 fl. oz) turkey or chicken stock
1 tbsp oyster sauce
1 tbsp soy sauce
1 tbsp cornstarch
Salt
Freshly ground black pepper
4 tbsp oil, for stir-frying
450 g (16 oz) button mushrooms, cut in half
1 stalk celery, roughly chopped
1 red pepper, roughly chopped
½ red onion, finely chopped
1 clove garlic, finely chopped
650 g (23 oz) white and dark cooked turkey meat, roughly chopped
2 carrots, roughly chopped
225 g (8 oz) bean sprouts
450 g (16 oz) pre-cooked chow mein noodles

1. To make the sauce, combine the stock, oyster sauce and soy sauce and whisk in the cornstarch. Season to taste.

2. Heat a wok or frying pan over a high heat. Add some of the oil and fry the mushrooms, then remove them from the pan and set aside. Add more oil to the pan and fry the celery and pepper. Remove them from the pan and mix with the mushrooms. Fry the onion and garlic in more oil. Add the turkey and fry for a minute or two, then return the mushrooms and other cooked vegetables to the pan along with the carrots and bean sprouts. Pour over the sauce and heat until it reaches boiling point. Turn off the heat, add the noodles and mix everything together thoroughly. Serve immediately.

Dear [name of relative with a wacky sense of humour],

Thank you so much for the Tony Blair mask/set of plastic comedy breasts/'I'm with stupid' T-shirt. It is hilarious! I laughed so hard, in fact, that I had to be hospitalized following a burst blood vessel. You truly are one of the great wits of our time. We would love to invite you round for Christmas next year so that you could entertain us with your amusing anecdotes and uncanny impersonation of Paul Daniels, but unfortunately we are emigrating to Australia.

Yours sincerely,

Let it Snow

A miracle has occurred and you've finally got the white Christmas you've been dreaming of, so wrap up warm, get yourself outside and have some fun! Here are some great suggestions for snowy activities:

❄ Play a game of snow tag. One person is 'It' and has to chase and catch the others, but they must only tread in the footprints made by those whom they're chasing. The first person to be caught is then 'It'.

❄ Make some snow ice cream. In a large bowl mix together: 1 tin of evaporated milk, 2 beaten eggs, 1½ teaspoons of vanilla extract and 200 g (7 oz) sugar. Go outside and gather together at least a gallon of fresh, clean snow. Gradually stir the snow into the mixture until you have the consistency you want and eat straight away.

❄ Build an outside snow lantern. Wait until dusk, then flatten the snow in the area you want to build your lantern and start making some tightly packed snowballs. Place the snowballs close together to form a circle on the ground, leaving a gap the width of one snowball. Now build a slightly smaller circle of snowballs on top of the first one, this time making the circle complete. Keep building the lantern up until it is the height you want, then top with a single snowball. Light a tea candle and push it through the gap in the first circle, so that it is in the middle of the lantern.

❄ Organize an epic snowball fight. Divide everyone into two teams and have each team build a snow fort – a low wall behind which players can shelter – facing each other but some distance away. A good tip to strengthen your fort is to pour cold water over it so that it ices over, but be careful not to spill any on the floor otherwise you will find it difficult to stand up! Next, set to work building up an arsenal of snowballs and store them behind your fort. Start the fight! The idea is to 'conquer' the enemy fort. Once a player has been hit by a snowball they are out and must retire from the game. If all players on a team are out, the opposing team claims the fort as their own.

❄ Create some snow art. Fill spray bottles with water and different food colourings. Flatten an area of snow and get creative.

True Christmas Stories: Bad Santas

Do sentimental images of rosy-cheeked children singing carols and happy families gathered round the fireplace make you sick to your stomach? Do you find the words 'bah' and 'humbug' escaping from your lips with alarming regularity at this time of year? Do you harbour deep misgivings about the bearded old man who sits your children on his knee and breaks into your house via the chimney? If so, you may want to consider joining The Cacophony Society.

The Cacophony Society – founded in 1986 – describes itself as 'a randomly gathered network of free spirits united in the pursuit of experiences beyond the pale of mainstream society.' In other words, its members are dedicated to causing as much mischief and mayhem as is humanly possible. Christmas is no exception. In fact, they positively embrace the idea of turning the season of goodwill to all into the season of drunkenness and misdemeanour. If you think this sounds a bit like any office Christmas party, think again.

In 1995, the society's San Francisco-based leader Michael Michel – known as 'M2' – and his sidekick, 'Reverend Al', organized the first SantaCon. More than fifty Santas, all the worse for wear, piled on to a hired bus and cavorted around San Francisco, storming hotels and shopping centres, mooning passers-by and stealing Christmas decorations. A good time was had by all, and the following year the number of rampaging Santas had doubled. This time it was Portland, Oregon that had the honour of hosting SantaCon, and the event was even more successful, with police in full riot gear being called out to control the increasingly deviant St Nicks. In 1997, more than 400 Santas brought parts of LA to a complete standstill as they whizzed around on skateboards and scooters and re-enacted the knife scene from *Rebel Without A Cause* – retitled *Rebels With A Claus* – and the event culminated in a riotous party in the sleaziest strip joint in town.

From then on, there was no stopping them, and annual SantaCon events are now held in cities all over the US, and even in Britain, New Zealand and Canada. All you need to join is an imaginative costume – the scarier or skimpier the better – and a passion for singing lewd carols, frightening children and abusing Christmas shoppers. Bewildered tourists are asked whether they've been 'naughty' or 'nice'; chants of 'Want to see the North Pole?' and 'Hell no, we won't ho!' fill the air; gifts of decapitated dolls and rusty batteries are generously handed out. It is, in short, good, clean, Christmas fun. Ho, ho, ho!

The Origins of Christmas Traditions

BOXING DAY

There is some debate as to the origins of Boxing Day, a holiday celebrated today by only a few English-speaking countries. It is generally accepted to have its roots in Britain, most probably in feudal times. The serfs would work on Christmas Day and be rewarded with a holiday the day after, when they would gather together and receive boxes filled with clothes and food from their lords to take home to their families. This practice continued in later years, when servants would present boxes to the master of the house when they arrived for work the day after Christmas and receive their end-of-year tips. The term 'Christmas box' is still used to refer to annual tips given to milkmen, postmen and so on.

Another theory is that the day after Christmas was traditionally the day when church donation boxes were opened and the money distributed to the needy.

Things to Do on Boxing Day

The presents have been opened, a vast quantity of food has been consumed and you're left with that post-Christmas feeling of anti-climax. What now? Perhaps consider the following:

❄ Book tickets to a pantomime. There's nothing quite like a good, hearty chorus of 'He's behind you!' to chase off the post-Christmas blues. Pick a good one, though, because when panto is bad, it is very bad indeed. Oh yes it is.

❄ Get to grips with all those wonderful gadgets you've been given and don't know how you've managed to live without. Read the manuals, insert batteries and tinker away to your heart's content.

❄ If the shopaholic in you is still clamouring for more, hit the sales, snap up some bargains and spend your gift vouchers.

❄ Go on a long winter walk to work off all those Christmas dinner calories.

❄ Organize a board game tournament. Choose four or five different games and play each one in turn for a set amount of time. Once that time is up, work out who was winning and award points for first place, second place and so on. Then move on to the next game. The person with the most points at the end wins the title of Board Game King or Queen.

❄ Get the kids to write their Thank You letters. Make it a fun activity rather than a chore by handing out card, glue, scissors, paints, glitter, stickers and so on, and getting them to make their own. The personalized touch will be much appreciated by the recipients, too.

❄ Have a leftovers party and invite any friends and neighbours whom you weren't able to see on Christmas Day. The one rule is: absolutely no more cooking! Ask everyone to bring a dish of leftovers.

❄ Keep that Christmas spirit of goodwill alive and volunteer to do something for someone less fortunate than you. Homeless shelters in particular are always busy during the Christmas season and welcome volunteers.

❄ Pamper yourself for a day. Gather together all those beauty products you've been given, soak in a hot, scented bath, give yourself a manicure, slap on a face mask and relax in front of the fire with a favourite book.

25 December
1979

The USSR airlifts an army to invade Afghanistan.

25 December
1989

Deposed Communist leader Nicolae Ceausescu and his wife Elena are executed in Romania.

Alternative Christmas Songs Lyrics

Annoy your family and friends by ruining their favourite seasonal jingles. Sing along using our alternative lyrics.

To be sung to the tune of 'Winter Wonderland':

Lacy things, the wife is missin',
Didn't ask her permission,
I'm wearin' her clothes,
Her silk pantyhose,
Walkin' round in women's underwear.

In the store, there's a teddy,
Little straps, like spaghetti,
It holds me so tight,
Like handcuffs at night,
Walkin' round in women's underwear.

To be sung to the tune of 'God Rest Ye Merry Gentlemen':

It was Christmas Day in the cookhouse,
The happiest day of the year,
Men's hearts were full of gladness,
And their bellies full of beer,
When up spoke Private Shorthouse,
His face as bold as brass,

141

Saying, 'You can take your Christmas pudding, Sarge,
And stick it up your . . .'

Tidings of comfort and joy, comfort and joy . . .

It was Christmas Day in the harem,
The eunuchs were standing around,
And hundreds of beautiful women
Were spread out on the ground;
Along came the bold bad Sultan
And surveyed his marble halls,
Said 'What do you want for Christmas, lads?'
And the eunuchs shouted . . .'

Tidings of comfort and joy, comfort and joy . . .

To be sung to the tune of 'Silent Night':
Silent fart, deadly fart,
Launched with stealth, a work of art,
Tears will well up and drop from your eyes,
It's an aroma that can't be disguised,
Try to breathe through your mouth,
Try to breathe through your mouth.

To be sung to the tune of 'White Christmas':
I'm dreaming of a quiet Christmas,
Well, maybe when the kids have grown,
No more fighting, swearing,
And music blaring,
At volumes hitherto unknown.

Top Ten Christmas Movies (2)

Part two of our list of films that are guaranteed to give you that warm, seasonal glow.

Holiday Inn (1942)

Perhaps not a film that immediately comes to mind as a Christmas classic, but it deserves a place in our top ten because of Irving Berlin's brilliant soundtrack, including the much-loved 'White Christmas', inimitably performed by Bing Crosby, and some wonderful song-and-dance numbers. Jim Hardy (Bing Crosby) gives up a successful stage career after his partner Ted Hanover (Fred Astaire) steals the love of his life, femme fatale Lila (Virginia Dale). However, he soon gets bored of life on his Vermont farm and decides, with the help of up-and-coming star Linda (Marjorie Reynolds), to convert it into an inn that is open only on public holidays. Things go swimmingly until Ted, having been dumped by Lila, shows up and sets his sights on Linda. Frothy holiday fun.

> **MEMORABLE QUOTE**
>
> TED: *I like it here, with you and Linda.*
> JIM: *And we love having you. When are you leaving?*

Home Alone (1990)

Home Alone may not be everyone's cup of tea, but its huge box-office success and enduring popularity earn it a place in our top ten. Eight-year-old Kevin McCallister (Macaulay Culkin) is inadvertently left behind when the rest of his family take off for a Christmas holiday in Paris and he is forced to deal with both the good and bad sides of his new independence. Throw in a couple of hapless burglars, Harry (Joe Pesci) and Marv (Daniel Stern), and some increasingly elaborate booby-traps and hilarity must surely ensue. Or not, depending on your point of view.

MEMORABLE QUOTE

KATE MCCALLISTER: *How could we do this? We forgot him.*

PETER MCCALLISTER: *We didn't forget him. We just miscounted.*

'I once bought my kids a set of batteries for Christmas with a note on it saying, "Toys not included."'
BERNARD MANNING

The Nightmare Before Christmas (1993)

If you've had your fill of the usual overly sentimental Christmas fare, then Tim Burton's typically quirky offering is the one for you. Jack Skellington is sick of Halloween Town and, enraptured by the cheery folk of Christmas Town, decides to take over the holiday festivities, with the help of various ghouls and goblins. Having had Santa kidnapped, he proceeds to inflict his own macabre version of Christmas on the world, which includes handing out demonic toys and shrunken heads to unsuspecting children, until he is finally forced to see the error of his ways. An animated masterpiece with some great musical numbers.

MEMORABLE QUOTE

JACK [singing]: *There's children throwing snowballs instead of throwing heads / They're busy building toys and absolutely no one's dead!*

'The Supreme Court has ruled that they cannot have a Nativity scene in Washington, D.C. This wasn't for any religious reasons. They couldn't find three wise men and a virgin.'

JAY LENO

How the Grinch Stole Christmas! (1966)

The 1966 animated version of the beloved Dr Seuss book beats hands-down the later live-action adaptation starring Jim Carrey. The text of the book is used throughout and is brought to life by some wonderful animation and musical numbers. The grumpy old Grinch is enraged by the cheery festivities of the inhabitants of Whoville and concocts a plan to stop Christmas from coming by stealing all their presents and decorations. He soon realizes, however, that Christmas is about more than material goods and redeems himself by returning his ill-gotten gains.

MEMORABLE QUOTE

NARRATOR: *He puzzled and puzz'd till his puzzler was sore.*
Then the Grinch thought of something he hadn't before!
'Maybe Christmas,' he thought, 'doesn't come from a store.'
'Maybe Christmas, perhaps, means a little bit more!'

The Santa Clause (1994)

A jolly family movie starring a perfectly cast Tim Allen as Scott Calvin, a divorced dad who is struggling to maintain a relationship with his young son Charlie (Eric Lloyd). On Christmas Eve, Scott and Charlie investigate a noise on the roof and startle Santa who falls to the ground and vanishes, leaving behind only his red suit. To please his son, Scott ill-advisedly dons the suit and the pair hop into the sleigh, whereupon they are whisked off to the North Pole, where Scott is informed that he will have to take over from Santa. At first, Scott dismisses the incident as a crazy dream, but is soon forced to come to terms with his new identity when he starts to put on weight at an alarming rate and struggles to keep his instantly regrowing long, white beard under control. Not exactly high-brow stuff, but great fun all the same.

MEMORABLE QUOTE

SCOTT:	*You know, you look pretty good for your age.*
LITTLE ELF JUDY:	*Thanks, but I'm seeing someone in Wrapping.*

UK Christmas
No. 1 Singles

Ever since the first UK singles chart was published in 1952, the Christmas No. 1 position has been the most hotly contested. Some genuine classics have made the grade, but the inclusion of the likes of Mr Blobby and Renée and Renato is baffling.

1952   Al Martino, 'Here In My Heart'

1953   Frank Laine, 'Answer Me'

1954   Winifred Atwell, 'Let's Have Another Party'

1955   Dickie Valentine, 'Christmas Alphabet'

1956   Johnnie Ray, 'Just Walkin' In The Rain'

1957   Harry Belafonte, 'Mary's Boy Child'

1958   Conway Twitty, 'It's Only Make Believe'

1959   Emile Ford & The Checkmates, 'What Do You Want To Make Those Eyes At Me For'

1960	Cliff Richard & The Shadows, 'I Love You'
1961	Danny Williams, 'Moon River'
1962	Elvis Presley, 'Return To Sender'
1963	The Beatles, 'I Want To Hold Your Hand'
1964	The Beatles, 'I Feel Fine'
1965	The Beatles, 'Day Tripper'
1966	Tom Jones, 'The Green Green Grass Of Home'
1967	The Beatles, 'Hello Goodbye'
1968	Scaffold, 'Lily The Pink'
1969	Rolf Harris, 'Two Little Boys'

1970	Dave Edmunds, 'I Hear You Knockin''
1971	Benny Hill, 'Ernie (The Fastest Milkman In The West)'
1972	Little Jimmy Osmond, 'Long-haired Lover From Liverpool'
1973	Slade, 'Merry Xmas Everybody'
1974	Mud, 'Lonely This Christmas'
1975	Queen, 'Bohemian Rhapsody'
1976	Johnny Mathis, 'When A Child Is Born'
1977	Wings, 'Mull Of Kintyre'
1978	Boney M, 'Mary's Boy Child'
1979	Pink Floyd, 'Another Brick In The Wall'

1980	St Winifred's School Choir, 'There's No One Quite Like Grandma'
1981	The Human League, 'Don't You Want Me?'
1982	Renée & Renato, 'Save Your Love'
1983	The Flying Pickets, 'Only You'
1984	Band Aid, 'Do They Know It's Christmas?'
1985	Shakin' Stevens, 'Merry Christmas Everyone'
1986	Jackie Wilson, 'Reet Petite'
1987	The Pet Shop Boys, 'Always On My Mind'
1988	Cliff Richard, 'Mistletoe and Wine'
1989	Band Aid II, 'Do They Know It's Christmas?'

1990	Cliff Richard, 'Saviour's Day'
1991	Queen, 'Bohemian Rhapsody'
1992	Whitney Houston, 'I Will Always Love You'
1993	Mr Blobby, 'Mr Blobby'
1994	East 17, 'Stay Another Day'
1995	Michael Jackson, 'Earth Song'
1996	The Spice Girls, '2 Become 1'
1997	The Spice Girls, 'Too Much'
1998	The Spice Girls, 'Goodbye'
1999	Westlife, 'I Have A Dream'

2000	Bob The Builder, 'Can We Fix It?'
2001	Robbie Williams & Nicole Kidman, 'Somethin' Stupid'
2002	Girls Aloud, 'Sound Of The Underground'
2003	Michael Andrews featuring Gary Jules, 'Mad World'
2004	Band Aid 20, 'Do They Know It's Christmas?'
2005	Shayne Ward, 'That's My Goal'
2006	Leona Lewis, 'A Moment Like This'

The Origins of Christmas Traditions

MISTLETOE

Like so many Christmas traditions that have survived through the ages, the hanging of mistletoe has its origins in pre-Christian times. The Celtic Druids and the ancient Greeks revered the plant, believing it had many mystical and healing properties. To them, its evergreen nature made it a symbol of prosperity and fertility, especially important in the bleak, hard winter months. The practice of hanging mistletoe indoors began in the Middle Ages, when branches were hung over doorways to ward off evil spirits.

The origins of the traditional kiss under the mistletoe are less clear. The mistletoe plant was associated with many ancient Greek fertility and marriage rites. To the Romans, mistletoe was a symbol of peace and in Norse legend the plant was associated with the goddess of love, Frigga or Freya. The modern practice began in eighteenth-century England. Young women who stood underneath the hanging mistletoe could not refuse a kiss, and if any unfortunate girl should remain unkissed, it was said that she would not marry within the next year.

A Child's Christmas in Wales

Published in 1955, *A Child's Christmas in Wales* is one of Dylan Thomas's most-loved pieces of writing: a nostalgic reminiscence of a Christmas that we all wish we could have, and somehow, despite its date, still evocative of the idiosyncrasies of each of our own Christmases today.

'And then the Presents, after the Christmas box. And the cold postman, with a rose on his button-nose, tingled down the tea-tray-slithered run of the chilly glinting hill. He went in his ice-bound boots like a man on fishmonger's slabs. He wagged his bag like a frozen camel's hump, dizzily turned the corner on one foot, and, by God, he was gone.'

'Get back to the Presents.'

'There were the Useful Presents: engulfing mufflers of the old coach days, and mittens made for giant sloths; zebra scarfs of a substance like silky gum that could be tug-o'-warred down to the galoshes; blinding tam-o'-shanters like patchwork tea cosies and bunny-suited busbies and balaclavas for victims of head-shrinking tribes; from aunts who always wore wool next to the skin there were moustached and rasping vests that made you wonder why the aunts had any skin left at all; and once I had a little crocheted nose bag from an aunt now, alas, no longer whinnying with us. And pictureless books in which small boys, though warned with quotations not to, *would* skate on Farmer Giles' pond and did and drowned; and books that told me everything about the wasp, except why.'

Dear [name of soon-to-be-ex husband],

Thank you so much for the dust buster/oven gloves/copy of How Clean Is Your House? It is so perceptive of you to realize that my burning ambition in life is to cater to your every need. A woman's place is, after all, in the kitchen, not at a fancy spa day or the opening night of an opera!

You may be wondering why I am writing you a Thank You note when we live in the same house. The fact is that we won't be for very much longer, and my lawyer has advised me to cease all verbal communication with you as of now. You will be hearing from him shortly. Merry Christmas!

Yours sincerely,

How to Pretend Christmas Isn't Happening

Year after year, you try your hardest to get into the spirit of Christmas. You struggle through crowds of hysterical last-minute shoppers; you put your back out lugging home the biggest tree money can buy, only to find it doesn't fit in your front room; you arrange your features into an expression of wonder and delight when you unwrap this year's novelty tie featuring Donald Duck or Bart Simpson; you pretend not to notice when Uncle Pete gets drunk and falls face-first into his Christmas pudding. But no matter how hard you try, you just can't cope with another Christmas. It's time to face facts. You are one of life's Scrooges, and that's OK. Here are some suggested coping mechanisms:

❋ Convert to a religion that doesn't celebrate Christmas. Better still, make up your own. There are many perks to being a cult leader.

❋ Embrace your Ebenezer tendencies! Wear severely cut, Victorian-style suits and walk around town with a sour expression on your face, shaking your cane and muttering at children or anyone else who looks like they might be having fun. Hire an impoverished yet good-hearted assistant and make him work long hours by candlelight while you sit counting your money on a pair of old-fashioned scales.

❄ Pretend that you are a moral campaigner, rather than the bitter old miser you are in reality, by loudly and argumentatively lecturing people about the evils of our consumer-led society and the cynical exploitation of the festive season.

❄ Make others feel guilty by proclaiming you are eschewing the frivolity of the season and instead will be spending Christmas volunteering in an African orphanage. Then draw the curtains, turn the heating up to tropical and revel in the glory of a family-free, money-saving Yuletide.

❄ Hibernate.

'It is, indeed, the season of regenerated feeling – the season for kindling, not merely the fire of hospitality in the hall, but the genial flame of charity in the heart.'

WASHINGTON IRVING

'Merry Christmas' Around the World

Language	'Merry Christmas'	Pronunciation
NORWEGIAN	God Jul	gord yule
PORTUGUESE	Feliz Natal	fleej nut-ahl
GERMAN	Fröhliche Weihnachten	frurlicka vy-nackten
CATALAN	Bon Nadal	bon nad-ahl
ROMANIAN	Crăciun Fericit	crae-chun fericit
WELSH	Nadolig Llawen	nadolig tlawen

157

Language	'Merry Christmas'	Pronunciation
ITALIAN	**Buon Natale**	bwon natarly
HUNGARIAN	**Kellemes Karácsonyi ünnepeket**	kel-le-mesh ko-raa-thonji ew-ne-pe-ket
POLISH	**Wesołych Świąt**	ve-so-wih shfyont
TURKISH	**Noel'iniz kutlu olsun**	no-e-lee-neez koot-loo ol-soon
VIETNAMESE	**Chúc bạn một mùa giáng sinh thật là vui vẽ**	chook ban momu yan sin that la voo vay
SPANISH	**Feliz Navidad**	felice navidath
LATVIAN	**Priecīgus Ziemassvētkus**	preah-tsee-guhs zea-mahs-svat-kuhs

25 December
1991

Mikhail Gorbachev resigns as President of the Soviet Union.

Language	'Merry Christmas'	Pronunciation
JAPANESE	メリークリスマス	merii kurisumasu
ARABIC	عيد ميلاد سعيد	eid milad saeed
CROATIAN	**Sretan Božić**	sre-than bau-zhee-ch
HINDI	क्रिस्मस की शुभ कामनाएं	christmas kee shubh kaamnaaye
FRENCH	**Joyeux Noël**	Shwoyure no-el

Acknowledgements

An extract from *A Child's Christmas in Wales* by Dylan Thomas (1993), published by Orion Children's Books, reprinted by kind permission of the Trustees for the copyrights of the late Dylan Thomas and of David Higham Associates Limited.

Grateful thanks to First Edition Translations Limited, and Daniela Fava and Erika Kumzaite in particular, for providing the material on pages 157 to 159, and to David Woodroffe for providing the illustrations on pages 25 to 26 and pages 112, 113, 114 (top) and 115.

Films: *Christmas Carol, A/Scrooge* (1951, George Minter Productions); *Holiday Inn* (1942, Paramount Pictures); *Home Alone* (1990, Hughes Entertainment and Twentieth Century Fox); *How the Grinch Stole Christmas!* (1966, MGM TV); *It's a Wonderful Life* (1946, Liberty Films); *Miracle on 34th Street* (1947, Twentieth Century Fox); *Nightmare Before Christmas, The* (1993, Skellington Productions Inc., Touchstone Pictures and Walt Disney Pictures); *Rudolph the Red-Nosed Reindeer* (1964, Rankin/Bass Productions); *Santa Clause, The* (1994, Walter Disney Pictures, Hollywood Pictures and Outlaw Productions); *Scrooged* (1988, Mirage Productions and Paramount Pictures).